provoking
THOUGHTS

provoking THOUGHTS

A Collection of Scriptures, Meditations and Prayers

Russell J. Levenson, Jr.

Insight Press
Covington, Louisiana

Provoking Thoughts: A Collection of Scriptures, Meditations and Prayers

Insight Press, Inc.
P.O. Box 5077, Covington, LA 70434

www.insightpress.net

Published 2009. Second printing, with changes 2015.
Printed in the United States of America

Cover artwork by Russell J. Levenson, Jr., oil on canvas, *"Sun Rising."*

Library of Congress Control Number: 2009911855

ISBN: 978–0–914520-59-7

To

Laura,

Evie, Jones and Luke

And to

My Parents

For your love, support and for

joining me on The Journey

"With Special Thanks..."

I am grateful to my favorite and best critic, my wife Laura, who read each meditation and made her own revisions. I also offer thanks to my children, Evie, Jones and Luke, who, for the season of my writing this book, did not have their Dad around as much; something I hope I have made up for since completing this piece.

I am grateful to the Communications Department of St. Martin's, and Maureen Vicent, for helping to edit, arrange and lay out each piece. Also, a "thank you" to Rebecca England and Justin Jacobson who fine-tuned with edits and a fresh layout for the second printing. To Dr. Fisher Humphreys and the leadership of *Insight Press,* and their support and encouragement of this book and others in this series. Also, my sincere thanks to the Rector's staff of St. Martin's: Carol Gallion, Brittney Jacobson and Allie Hippard, who help me guard and protect my schedule for projects like this one.

Lastly, I am deeply appreciative of my mentor and friend, Lord George Carey, who encouraged me in this project. His words will offer you a foreword to this traveling companion.

— Russ Levenson

Contents

Before We Begin...

"Follow Me..."

— Matthew 4:19

St. Augustine wrote that his heart was restless until it found its rest in God. C.S. Lewis once spoke of the human heart as having a "God-shaped hole" that remained incomplete until God filled that hole.

Lord George Carey, the author of the foreword for this little book, wrote *"We are living in a fragmented society whose most serious dislocation is between the human and the divine."*[1]

The ache of the human heart has always been to be made whole. The thrust of the Christian hope is that it can only come to that wholeness by being connected in a personal relationship with God, through Christ. This book is intentionally written as perhaps one more avenue towards deepening, strengthening, and for some, maybe birthing such a relationship.

It is crafted as a Lenten companion to begin with Ash Wednesday and carry us through Easter Day with one additional meditation—but one does not have to limit its use to Lent. All of us need times of

1 George Carey, *I Believe* (Harrisburg: Morehouse, 1991) 20.

reflection and renewal, and that certainly does not have to be limited to a particular season or time of the year.

A few caveats before you begin. Obviously, as with any writer's work, I offer an understanding of God and His redemptive work in Christ through my own lens. That lens is molded by a firm commitment to the authority of Holy Scripture; the traditions of the church; dozens of mentors, teachers and writers; and finally, through my years of service as an ordained priest. I write from the perspective of one who believes in the central truths of Christianity, so it will soon become clear that some things are assumed in my writing. Particularly, that the reader will either have an ongoing relationship with God or is, at the very least, interested in having one.

The reader will also find that I make use of the wisdom of others and of narrative stories to help build each meditation. I also write from a certain perspective because I have inherited a tradition that refers to the Divine much more in masculine terms, rather than feminine or neuter. I honor that tradition in my writing here. I do not necessarily believe that God is simply a "great, big man" in the heavens; at times, God is referred to with feminine and even androgynous descriptions. Nevertheless, when our Lord referred to God, it was primarily as our "heavenly Father," and I must, out of my own reverence for that kind of description, follow His lead.

Lastly, let me offer a few words about the methodology. Each meditation is introduced by a title, a Scripture I have selected, the meditation itself, a photo or two, a provoking thought and a prayer either from the Church's tradition or my own hand.

Living in Texas, I have many opportunities to use shotguns. When I was a teenager, I was somewhat of a marksman with a rifle. The difference with a shotgun is that you have a greater chance of hitting

some target with the wide spread of buckshot. With a rifle, the goal is to hit the bull's-eye of only one target.

In my writing here, I have taken a shotgun approach. I am assuming that my readers will come from different places. Some of these meditations may appeal and some may not; some will apply and others will not. While there may be sections of meditations that seem to fit together, for the most part there is no stair-step approach here. Take each meditation as it is intended and prepared—with the hope that some aspect of each might help in making that connection between your need and the provision of God in Christ.

I like the words Jesus used to inaugurate His relationship with each disciple, *"Follow Me."* Not a command, but an invitation. They did not have to follow, but they were lovingly invited to do so. It is my profound hope that some piece of this work will help each reader to do just that.

Almighty God,
By Whose spoken Word,
All things came into being;
Speak to us now,
That we may be inspired by your Holy Spirit,
And drawn to follow and proclaim
Jesus Christ as our Lord and our Savior.[2]

—The Reverend Dr. Russell J. Levenson, Jr.
Rector, St. Martin's Church
Houston, Texas
Lent, 2010

2 A prayer written by Russell J. Levenson, Jr.

Please Join Us

by The Most Reverend and Right Honorable
Dr. George L. Carey
103rd Archbishop of Canterbury, 1991-2002

When I was reading the draft of Russell's excellent book of meditations, I was reminded of a saying that I read many years ago. The writer observed that the two great discoveries that modern people longed for was *"light on the mystery of life and power for the mastery of life."*

Who can doubt that as a fact? We cussed human beings long to understand and we are constantly pushing out the boundaries of knowledge. In the last one hundred years so much has been discovered in medicine, astronomy and science generally. As a consequence, life has become, for many of us in the West, much more comfortable and enjoyable. If you ever have cause to doubt this, ask yourself if you would prefer to have dental work done by a 19th century dentist with his tools of the trade rather than your current dentist!

And this is where the second longing comes in—we know so much more, yet it has not exactly led to moral enhancement. Life in many parts of the world is more dangerous. Sadly, London, where I grew up, is today a place where certain parts are "no go" areas. But that was not the case when I was a youngster. In spite of the poverty engendered by two world wars, a strong feeling of community existed and people cared for one another. Winston Churchill put it so well towards the end of his life when he said, *"Man's domination now extends over every part of nature, except over himself."*

Again I ask, who can doubt it? We resist failure in every part of life, yet seem to assume that it is inevitable in our personal lives. We seem to take it for granted that we shall never overcome feelings of inadequacy, guilt or moral failure.

This is where Dr. Levenson's book speaks so powerfully to the heart of contemporary people. He takes us on a journey from Lent to Easter Day; from death to life, from despair to hope and from tragedy to triumph. I love the natural, easy way he writes, surely the mark of someone who is a born communicator! Furthermore, he does not duck the tough questions as some preachers tend to do, neither does he offer simplistic solutions to the moral demands that come our way day after day. Instead, he reminds us why being a Christian is the most wonderful thing in the whole world.

I commend this book to you all. Eileen and I intend to use it throughout Lent because it is so accessible and easy to read at the beginning of the day. Join us by doing so and, you never know, it just might help us all find *"power for the mastery of life."*

Seeing Death

"Remember how short my time is—For what vanity you have created all mortals! Who can live and never see death? Who can escape the power of Sheol?"

— Psalm 89:47-48

In the mid-1600s, the "Black Death" or "Black Plague" wiped out nearly one third of the population of Europe and the British Isles. There was great speculation about what caused the plague. One theory was the thick blankets of soot and ash which filled the London skyline.

People began to carry flower petals in their pockets thinking that might ward off the disease. Groups of victims who were still able to stand were taken outside treatment centers, and while holding hands, they would walk in circles around rose gardens, breathing deeply the freshness of blooming flowers. We all know the little verse that went with this practice,

Ring around the rosie,
A pocket full of posies.
Ashes, ashes, we all fall down.

But of course, they were wrong, and people continued to "fall down" until the real cause of the sickness was determined—flea bites from diseased rats.

Death is a hard thing to ponder, but it is a good thing to ponder. It is not unique to our age that people try to postpone or avoid death. Charlatans were selling life-lengthening tonic water almost as soon as bottles could be crafted, and De Soto was not the first to seek the mythical "fountain of youth."

All that has been dressed up a bit now. One only has to turn on late-night television to be reminded there are new pills, herbs, formulas, weight-loss programs and exercise machines that claim to take the years away. Plastic surgery in the western world has grown into a veritable industry. But if we think any of these offers or procedures will protect us from death, it is no different from placing posies in our pockets as a superstitious attempt to escape death's clutches. The truth is, we all fall down.

"Remember you are dust and to dust you shall return," are the most familiar words spoken during the Ash Wednesday services in several Christian traditions. The words are a reminder that we are not just born of the dust of the earth, but we will return to that dust as well.[1]

It could be quite depressing if it all ended there. But the gift of death is a reminder of the gift of life itself, of the need to make the most of life while one lives it, of the need to live life as it should be lived.

We are, all of us, "terminally ill." None of us can escape the power of what the Psalmist calls *Sheol,* or the grave. If that is true, if we know there is a finish line toward which we are all running, whether we like it or not, then should it not drive us to make the very most and best of our lives? By "most," I mean should we not learn to feed ourselves with those things that will bless us in every way—physically, emotionally, mentally, spiritually? By "best," should we not seek to live moral, ethical lives? Lives of peace and harmony with God, with our neighbor, with ourselves?

Many see death as an enemy to be avoided. Perhaps it can be a companion along life's journey to remind us to make the most and the best of it.

1 Genesis 2:7.

Provoking Thought

If there was one phrase by which you would be remembered, what words would be used?

A Prayer for Reflection

Glorious God, give me grace to amend my life, and to have an eye to mine end without grudge of death, which to them that die in thee, good Lord, is the gate of a wealthy life. And give me, good Lord, an humble, lowly, quiet, peaceable, patient, charitable, kind, tender, and pitiful mind, with all my works and all my words and all my thoughts, to have a taste of thy holy, blessed Spirit. Give me, good Lord, a full faith, a firm hope, and a fervent charity, a love to thee incomparable above the love to myself. Give me, good Lord, a longing to be with thee, not for the avoiding of the calamities of this world, nor so much for the attaining of the joys of heaven, as for a very love of thee. And bear me, good Lord, thy love and favour, which thing my love to theeward, were it never so great, could not but thy great goodness deserve. These things, good Lord, that I pray for, give me thy grace to labour for. Amen.

Sir Thomas More, d. 1535
Offered prior to his execution[2]

2 Michael Counsell, comp. *2000 Years of Prayer* (Harrisburg: Morehouse, 1999) 174-175.

Sinning Business

"For there is no distinction, since all have sinned and fall short of the glory of God..."

— Romans 3:22-23

"I am a sinner." It is out, and now you know. I hate admitting that, and even worse, saying it aloud. But it is a truth I cannot deny. I suppose if the Apostle Paul can admit it in his letter to the Romans, I should be willing to do the same.

Over the years, I have presided at many religious services that began by dawn's early light. Between waking and kneeling for the confession during those services, there is hardly a chance to get into any of the "sinning business." I have spent the majority of my adult life *in* this religious business and I still

find that every time I kneel, my sin is staring me in the face. And every time I get to that moment, I realize that behind every confession the culprit is *me!*

I would like to think I am not too self-centered. But I do struggle to not overfeed that one in the mirror. I wonder if you do, too? For example, when looking at your new photos, at whom do you first look? Is it not yourself? "How did *I* turn out?" "Why did *I* wear that shirt?" "*I* should have worn sunglasses!" After that, perhaps your eyes turn to your loved ones, your children or the friend with whom you traveled.

We are naturally drawn to ourselves, and that is not all bad! We are to love ourselves, our dear Lord said, but then at the same time, we are also told to deny ourselves when our "selves" get in the way of loving God or our neighbor.[1]

Life would be so much easier if all we had to do was carry out the "loving self" bit and let the rest alone. Too much self leads to one road and one road alone—sin in all of its forms.

The overindulgent love of self is that thing to which the Dark One appealed. *"Eat and you will be like God,"* the serpent said to the first human couple.[2] The temptation was not in eating a Granny Smith, but the desire to "be like God." And when the temptation was accepted, all the evil began and continues to this day. The appeal then was to *"put yourself on the throne and forget about God ruling your lives."* How did it turn out? Read today's paper or watch the evening news to see what happens when we try to run things. Suddenly, taking on the role of God seems to be way above our pay grade.

Thus, we must still work on giving the "self" over to God in Christ more and more. Christians believe that is the only path to wholeness. It is why Jesus often described the whole journey of Christianity as starting with a kind of new birth. He called it *"born again."*[3] For the fullness of God's presence to begin in me, "I" have to die and be "born anew."

For goodness' sake, please do not let those words alarm you! Use whatever metaphor works for you like "converted," "seeing the light," "renewed" or "awakened."

1 Luke 9:23; 10:27.
2 Genesis 3:5.
3 John 3:3.

John Mason wrote, *"They that deny themselves for Christ shall enjoy themselves in Christ."*[4] The point is to deny the self and find your true self. Allow the self to die and commence the life God wants for you. And that is a miracle to behold indeed.

Perhaps it is time to get in touch with your*self* and see how much it might be getting in the way of the God*self* that needs to be born in you. If you are anything like me, it has a tendency to get in the way. All the more to give to God in Christ. All the more for which to be thankful that the same Christ is willing to accept it, mend it and give it back anew.

Provoking Thought

What is the first selfish trait that is interfering in your relationship with God and others? Ask God to help you release it into His loving and redemptive care.

A Prayer for Reflection

Lord Jesus, here I am, this mixed up tent of broken poles and torn fabric; this vessel with cracks and chips; this all-too-human and frail child of your own creation. And yet I have abused Your gift of life, taken advantage of the freedom You have awarded me, betrayed Your mercy once again. I have sinned, my heavenly Savior—in thought and word and deed, against You, my neighbor and myself. I have sinned deliberately, and I have sinned in ignorance; I have both chosen my sin and fallen into it. And now the burden of my wrong choices and the weight of their guilt is too much. Forgive me, dear Lord; forgive me and make me new. Empty me of all things impure and unholy, and fill me afresh with Your Holy Spirit that all broken places may be restored, and all sin be wiped away. Forgive me, O Lord, forgive me and make me new. Amen.

— RJL+[5]

4 Martin H. Manser, comp. *The Westminster Collection of Christian Quotations* (Louisville: Westminster John Knox, 2001) 335.

5 RJL+ denotes a prayer written by Russell J. Levenson, Jr.

Do Over

"Very truly, I tell you, no one can see the kingdom of God without being born from above."

—John 3:3

When I was a kid, and before the age of hyper-competitive children's sports, it was not uncommon on the ball field to call for a "do over." What that meant, especially in T-Ball, was that the batter might have tapped the ball without intending to hit it, and he did not want it to be counted against him as an attempt to smack it out of the park! Now I rarely smacked it out of the park, but I was usually always grateful for a chance to "do over," give it another try, without having my past mistakes count against me.

In the rather well-known scene from John's Gospel mentioned above, we find Jesus having a meeting with a major religious leader named Nicodemus. Nicodemus was a good and godly man. He knew his Scriptures, practiced his religion and was not afraid to spar with someone like Jesus. But he was also spiritually hungry. All his attention to the rules of religion was not scratching a deeper spiritual itch. Jesus hit the nail on the proverbial head. Jesus was trying to get Nicodemus to see that his eyes and heart were focused on the Law and not the Lawgiver. Jesus told Nicodemus he would have to be *"born from above."* Nicodemus needed a "do over."

He needed not just greater understanding, but new eyes, a new mind, a new heart and a new self. What this required was a kind of internal, global shift in the tectonic plates of his being. He needed to be born again, as some biblical translations put it.

As I wrote in the last meditation, do not let those two words frighten you. If you think on it long enough, who would not like a "do over "in some area of their life? The husband who has betrayed his wife? The employee who has stolen or the employer who has treated one harshly? The mother who has spent more time disciplining her children than loving and accepting them? The teenager caught in a web of alcohol or drug addiction? The prisoner who acted in haste and without forethought? The friend who has neglected?

Maybe the opportunity for a "do over" is not limited to one event, but to one's entire way of seeing things, and perhaps, even one's entire life. That is the invitation Jesus issues to Nicodemus, and to each of us. New life finds its origin, birthplace if you will, not in religion but in relationship. Religion or the practice thereof, is usually an expression of our relationship. Later in John's Gospel, Jesus teaches that *"All who see the Son and believe in Him may have eternal life."*[1] John Newton once said, *"Christianity is not a system of doctrine but a new creature."*

We all know we cannot change the past, but what Jesus always offers us is the opportunity to start afresh. The invitation to be born anew is much more powerful than the simple permission for a "do over."

---

1 John 6:40.

It is the opportunity to have a whole new life—a life grounded not in stifling expectations of perfection, but in giving room for another try with God as your companion along the way.

So who is up for a spiritual "do over"? I know I am, how about you?

Provoking Thought

What area of your life, past mistake, sin or relationship would you like to do over? Can you offer that into the care of Christ who offers you new birth? Can you accept that gift?

A Prayer for Reflection

O God, the King eternal, whose light divides the day from the night and turns the shadow of death into the morning: drive far from us all wrong desires, incline our hearts to keep your law, and guide our feet into the way of peace; that having done your will with cheerfulness during the day, we may, when night comes, rejoice to give you thanks; through Jesus Christ our Lord. Amen.

— William Reed Huntingdon, d. 1909[2]

2 *The Book of Common Prayer* (New York: Church Hymnal Corporation, 1979) 56.

Forgive Us Our Sins...

"Forgive us our debts, as we also have forgiven our debtors."

— Matthew 6:12

When one ponders, as we have been in these last few meditations, things like death and how we live our lives, it is not long before the issue of forgiveness rises to the surface.

When the New Testament described one's sin, many might have heard an analogy to archery. For Jesus' earliest followers, to sin was to "miss the mark," as an archer might attempt, but fail, to hit the bull's-eye. Of course, sometimes the archer hits it dead on, but that is usually the exception and not the rule. We modern archers know that most of the time we miss the mark. Many of our lives are peppered with the dark grains of sin. If that is the case, how can forgiveness become more than a word?

Every now and then I read of a modern, often proud, secularist or atheist who boldly proclaims the concept of a need for forgiveness to be outdated. A modern mantra of "live as you please," taken to the extreme, means there really is no right and wrong, as long as you are happy with your life. But live long enough, and it is not hard to begin to feel what can only be described as a kind of burden of guilt. In an interview with the BBC shortly before her death, well-known secular humanist, Marghanita Laski said, *"What I envy most about you Christians is your forgiveness; I have nobody to forgive me."*[1]

John Claypool reflects on this rather well when he writes, *"You cannot ignore sin just because it is distasteful. Disposing of guilt by evasion is a way of dealing with it, but an utterly disastrous one; you might as well gather up the termites you find in the living room and deal with them by turning them loose in your basement!"*[2] So how do we begin to wrestle with this issue of forgiveness?

Well, Christians affirm a kind of universal forgiveness offered in the death of Jesus Christ. This is hard for us to understand and even embrace for several reasons. Once we have gotten past the naïve belief that when we hurt others it really does not matter and there is no need for their forgiveness, then it is a very human tendency to try to "pay up" for our mistakes. That is why in the Lord's Prayer, the request "forgive us" is sometimes accompanied by the word debt. A debt is something that has to be paid. But who pays this one?

Perhaps one of the real misunderstandings about Christianity is that our acceptance by God is based on some kind of great ledger in the sky. If the good marks outweigh the bad then you pass the test (bull's-eye!), but if the bad outweigh the good, the trap door opens and down you go (you miss the mark!). That kind of Christianity is not based on who you are, but on what you do. And if God's love depends on what we do, then you and I are no doubt already behind the curve. But if it is based on who we are, then there may just be a chance, if we understand who we are. And who is that?

In the last meditation we looked at the conversation taking place between Jesus and Nicodemus. Here Jesus tried to bring it all home for His new disciple with some words well known to Christians and non-Christians alike: *"For God so loved the world that He gave His only Son, so that everyone who believes in Him may not perish but may have eternal life. Indeed, God did not send the Son into the world to condemn the world, but in order that the world might be saved through Him."*[3]

1 John R. W. Stott, *The Contemporary Christian: Applying God's Word to Today's World* (New York: InterVarsity, 1995) 48.
2 John Claypool, *The Light Within You: Looking at Life Through New Eyes* (Waco: Word Books, 1983) 186.
3 John 3:16-17.

Now all of that love, life, non-condemnation and promise of salvation business sounds more like a God who is offering forgiveness, does it not?

So where *do* I take my sins? I take them to the Cross of Jesus Christ. On the Cross Jesus was willing to absorb all the evil, sin and guilt of the world; He was willing to take them on Himself. Theologians call this "substitutionary atonement," meaning the atonement that might be paid through any other form is transferred, substituted by a stand-in, Jesus Christ. This is why Jesus' first cousin, John the Baptist, called Christ, *"the Lamb of God who takes away the sin of the world!"*[4]

So perhaps the place to begin understanding forgiveness is to give up some old misconceptions about it: that we somehow pay the price for our own sins, or that it is unnecessary, or that God is more like a celestial accountant than a heavenly parent.

I will unpack this more in the pages to come, but for now, consider letting go of the Divine Accountant and letting the Loving God take hold of you.

Provoking Thought

When you read or hear the word "guilt" what first comes to mind? And the word "forgiveness"?

A Prayer for Reflection

O My Lord, since it seems you are determined to save me, I ask that you may do so quickly. And since you have decided to dwell within me, I ask that you clean your house, wiping away all grime of sin.

— Teresa of Avila, d. 1582

4 John 1:29.

As We Seek Forgiveness

"If we say that we have no sin, we deceive ourselves, and the truth is not in us. If we confess our sins, He who is faithful and just will forgive us our sins and cleanse us from all unrighteousness."

— I John 1:8-9

In the last meditation, I shared the Christian belief that the answer for the "sin of the world," in the words of John the Baptist, was Christ Jesus. He is that Lamb that takes away the sin. As the Apostle Timothy writes, *"The saying is sure and worthy of full acceptance, that Christ Jesus came into the world to save sinners..."*[1] I will come back to that in a few pages.

1 I Timothy 1:15.

While it is true that Jesus forgives sin (and all sin), most of us still have to deal with our own particular offenses. In short, it is one thing to feel sorry about one's actions, but it is another thing to actually say "I'm sorry." Since the beginning of creation, part of the pathway toward embracing the full gift of God's forgiveness is summed up in one word, *confession.*

Confession is that act of really letting go of the spiritual, physical, emotional and mental sickness that often accompanies our sinful actions. I still remember years ago when a friend of mine became

deeply mired in a pattern of deceitful and sinful behavior. For no apparent reason, both of her hands began to swell. She sought out her physician, who ran tests with no firm results or explanation. It finally occurred to my friend that she had been carrying the burden of her sin for too long. As she began to let go of her sin through her confession, the swelling disappeared almost as soon as it had appeared.

Part of our engagement with the Lord's prayer that God would *"forgive us our debts as we forgive,"* is to actually receive God's forgiveness. It is quite hard for the light that forgiveness brings to find its way in if we have not opened ourselves to let the darkness out. This light is called confession, and it happens in all kinds of ways. In many Jewish and Protestant denominations, congregations corporately confess as part of their regular worship. The Roman tradition requires not only corporate confession, but private confession as well. For many Christians (perhaps most), the simple act of getting on one's knees at the end of the day and unpacking one's heart is a powerful example of confession. Whatever the route, why not take it now?

Provoking Thought

Call to mind a sin or sins that you have carried too long. Can you use the prayer below to let go of that sin through God's gift of confession?

A Prayer for Reflection

Jesus said, There is joy among the angels of God
Over one sinner who repents.
Come to me all who labour and are heavy laden
And I will give you rest.
God has promised forgiveness to all who truly repent,
Turn to Christ in faith, and are themselves forgiving.
In silence we call to mind our sins.

Silence is observed here.

Merciful God,
we have sinned
in what we have thought and said,
in the wrong we have done
and in the good we have not done.
We have sinned in ignorance:
We have sinned in weakness:
We have sinned through our own deliberate fault.
We are truly sorry.
We repent and turn to you.
Forgive us, for our Saviour Christ's sake,
And renew our lives to the glory of your name. Amen.

— *He Karakia Mihinare o Aotearoa* (1989)
from a *New Zealand Prayer Book*[2]

2 Counsell 503.

As We Forgive Those Who Sin Against Us

"Then Peter came and said to Him, 'Lord, if another member of the church sins against me, how often should I forgive? As many as seven times?'
Jesus said to him, 'Not seven times, but, I tell you, seventy times seven.'"

— Matthew 18:21-22

In some ways, this little scene between Peter and Jesus is comical. Anyone who has had to deal with children has probably encountered the crying child trying to justify his or her naughty behavior with the words, *"They did it first!"* No doubt, Peter was trying to find some way of wiggling out of forgiving even one more time. And yet, Jesus does not let him off the hook. *"You are not to forgive just seven times, but seventy times seven!"* As you may know, in Jesus' day, seven was a symbol, not just a number. It often had an eternal, endless quality to it. So really, Jesus is not telling Peter that forgiveness runs out after the 490th time—but to forgive, and forgive and forgive!

Now why should we do that? Well, one reason is clear. Jesus tells us plainly, *"Forgive us our sins as we forgive those who sin against us."*[1] It is

1 Matthew 6:12.

not only Jesus' instruction to forgive, but a warning that unless we forgive, we will lock God's forgiveness out of our own hearts. That may seem cruel, perhaps conditional and harsh, but consider the reasoning.

If we deny forgiveness, we are allowing all our pain to give way to anger, resentment and even hatred, festering within us like a poison. Frederick Buechner writes with great skill about anger's effect on the human soul:

> *Of the Seven Deadly Sins, anger is possibly the most fun. To lick your wounds, to smack your lips over grievances long past, to roll over your tongue the prospect of bitter confrontations still to come, to savor to the last toothsome morsel—both the pain you are given and the pain you are giving back—in many ways it is a feast fit for a king. The chief drawback is that what you are wolfing down is yourself. The skeleton at the feast is you.*[2]

At this point, it may be tempting to allow the *"Yes, buts"* to gather! *"Yes, but can we forgive if our enemy does not repent?"* Jesus might answer, *"Can your enemy repent unless you are willing to forgive?"* Jesus on the Cross prayed that His enemies might be forgiven while they were still intent on His death.

"Yes, but you don't know how badly I have been hurt." That may be true. It might be that you do not know how badly you have hurt your offender. Nevertheless, we pray, *"forgive us our sins, as we forgive those who sin against us."*

"Yes, but what if we forgive and they hurt us again?" Jesus says forgive *"seventy times seven."*

2 Frederick Buechner, *Wishful Thinking: A Theological ABC* (San Francisco: Harper & Row, 1973) 2.

If we want mercy, we must be willing to shell it out. Our only other choice is to let all the pain, wounds and resentment continue to have power over us.

Offering forgiveness really is freeing. How long do you want the words *anger, resentment* or *grudge* to be part of your heart's vocabulary? Better, is it not, to let them go, so that not only have you given mercy, but you have made room in your own life for it to enter in as well?

Provoking Thought

Who do you need to forgive today? Why are you waiting?

A Prayer for Reflection

"O Lord, remember not only the men and women of good will, but also those of ill will. But do not remember all the suffering they have inflicted on us; remember the fruits we have bought, thanks to this suffering—our comradeship, our loyalty, our courage, our generosity, the greatness of heart which has grown out of all of this, and when they come to judgment let all the fruits which we have borne be their forgiveness."

— This prayer was written by an unknown prisoner at Ravensbruck Concentration Camp and left by the body of a dead child[3]

3 Mary Batchelor, comp. *The Doubleday Prayer Collection* (New York: Doubleday, 1997) 50-51.

As We Forgive Ourselves

"...as far as the east is from the west, so far He removed our transgressions from us."

— Psalm 103:12

Having touched on forgiveness in general, that is the need to seek forgiveness by saying "I am sorry" and the need to forgive others by extending mercy, there is one more "directional" imperative to consider—forgiving *ourselves.*

That concept may seem a bit out of place. If we have sought forgiveness from God, is it not God's business, and not ours, to forgive? Well, yes and no. God does seek to forgive and God does forgive. As noted in the Psalm above, the forgiveness He offers takes our wrongdoing and flings it as far as the east is from the west! But just because God has forgiven us, that does not mean we *have forgiven ourselves.*

If we are earnest and give our sins to God, we are told He wipes them away, as if they had never existed. If God can forgive us, why do we not forgive ourselves?

Guilt is a great tool at times. It can bring us to our knees, pleading for the mercy of God when we need it. But once God has forgiven us, we need to let go of our guilt. If it sticks around, you can be sure it is not of God. It is being used by the evil one to drive you down into despair, into a feeling of unworthiness such that you do not even want to be in the presence of God.

One of my closest friends, a psychiatrist, was having lunch with a colleague who was the administrator of an inpatient mental health facility. He told my friend, *"You know, if I could ever get two messages into the psyche and heart of each of these patients, I could release most of them today."* What are those messages? He said they were simple, *"You are forgiven and you are loved."*

"Forgive us our sins, as we forgive ourselves" really is perhaps the last step we take in dealing with our personal sin and its traveling companion, guilt. However, there is another good reason to learn to accept God's forgiveness. It is that we will also learn to spend less time on how "I" feel all the time, and more time on how others feel. Accepting forgiveness allows us to be more merciful to others.

Forgive us our sins, as we seek forgiveness, as we forgive others and as we forgive ourselves. What has God chosen to do with the sin you have brought to Him for forgiveness? He has forgiven you! Why not do the same?

Provoking Thought

God has forgiven you, but have you forgiven yourself? Take some time and reflect on God's forgiveness. Take some time and receive it, not just for a moment, but for all the days ahead. It is gone... completely.

A Prayer for Reflection

Lord Jesus, you taught us to forgive others, just as you forgave those who treated you badly. Help us to remember how much you have forgiven us and to be willing to forgive those who hurt us. For your sake, Amen.

— A children's prayer[1]

1 Edna and Jack Young, *Praying with Juniors* (Surrey, UK: National Christian Education Council, 1968).

The Burnt-Over Place

"Out of his anguish he shall see light; he shall find satisfaction through his knowledge. The righteous one, my servant, shall make many righteous, and he shall bear their iniquities."

— Isaiah 53:11

Among Isaiah's many writings are included several images of the "Suffering Servant," foreshadowing and prophesying the death of Jesus for the sin of all humankind. This act of Jesus making sinful people righteous is called justification.

What this means, in very practical terms, is that through Jesus the payment for our sins has been paid. Once forgiven, there is no "payback" to be made on your part for the sin you may have committed. Furthermore, there is nothing you can do as it relates to God to further take care of the problem of sin. This of course, does not mean there may not be some clean-up necessary as it relates to our earthly journey. Forgiveness of the tax cheat by God does not mean they will not have to deal with the IRS. Forgiveness of the adulterer by God does not mean that the pain of the offended will be wiped away, and so on. No, justification in God's eyes means simply that in the last court of appeal (which is certainly His), with the gavel's fall comes the two words, "not guilty."

A clergy friend of mine told me of a time when two of his church members were out duck hunting in south Georgia. They were surprised by the onset of a fast-moving brushfire and believed that they had no escape, until one of them came up with an idea. He searched his pack for some matches, and started a much smaller fire in their midst. After a few minutes, the two of them were sitting in the middle of a black circle where the brush under their feet had already been burned. They covered their mouths with wet cloths and waited for the oncoming blaze. When it arrived, the fire moved right around them—fire would not pass where it had already passed.

The Cross of Christ, the death of the Suffering Servant, is that "burned-over" place. Punishment cannot be revisited in a place where punishment has already occurred. When we come to terms with that, there is a real freedom in knowing that while we may still have to deal with some of the earthly challenges around our sinful behavior, like confession, reconciliation and restitution, in God's eyes the price has been paid.

Provoking Thought

What things do you do to try to win God's justification? If you have been justified by His death on the Cross, what more can you do than be thankful? Take some time right now and offer that thanks.

A Prayer for Reflection

O God, before Whose face we are not made righteous even by being right; free us from the need to justify ourselves by our own anxious striving, that we may be abandoned to faith in you alone, through Jesus Christ. Amen.

— RJL+

The Waiting Game

"Wait for the Lord; be strong, and let your heart take courage; wait for the Lord!"

— Psalm 27:14

I have spent a good bit of this particular day waiting. I waited on the cable guy to come and fix our cable. I waited on the electrician to come and repair some outlets that had stopped working. On the way to the doctor's office, I had to wait in traffic and when I arrived at the doctor's office, I waited some more.

Waiting is hard for most people, especially for those in the very much industrialized and connected west. We have invented several ways to fill up the "dead space" of waiting. Do you agree? When is the last time you checked your cell phone while waiting at a red light? How many times have you checked your email today?

Our Judeo-Christian faith has a great deal of waiting in it. In the opening chapters of Genesis, we find that the first real outcome of Adam's disobedience was that he would no longer have food at the snap of his fingers, but would have to toil the land *"by the sweat of your face."*[1] In other words, he would have to wait for what he wanted.

1 Genesis 3:17-19.

The whole history of Judaism was wrapped up in waiting for the Messiah. Moses spent forty years waiting in the desert before he could lead the Jews into the Promised Land. Jesus spent forty days waiting in the desert before He began His ministry. Once Jesus came, the whole history of Christians became, and remains, focused on waiting for His return.

Waiting is very hard. Waiting on the exam grades to be posted. Waiting on the call after the job interview. Waiting for the wedding to be over. Waiting for the baby to arrive. Waiting on the diagnosis. Waiting for the pain to stop. Sometimes we call this the "waiting game," though it is usually not a very fun game.

There are, however, at least two things we can do with the waiting game. The first is to settle into it. Any physician would tell you that to stop your rapid pace, take a breather and close your eyes is a good thing for your physical health. The same is true of your spiritual health. Stop. Just stop. Use that time to think on the day gone by, the moment you are in or the things yet to come. Pray for others—for yourself, for the man in traffic next to you, the woman in line in front of you—just pray. I would bet Moses did some of that during those forty years, and I bet that is about all Jesus did during His forty days.

The second way to play the waiting game is to embrace what it may be all about—turning more to God. When David penned the words from the opening Scripture, it was a poem to his reader, but perhaps also to himself. He had enemies galore and wanted protection from them. He did not want God to forget him. He had to wait, and when he did, he also realized that he was waiting *on the Lord*. David's inability to control his own situation, to speed things up or end the waiting game, *made him turn to the Lord.*

So maybe waiting is not all that bad. Maybe it is actually a gift sent from God; a gift to give you a bit more time to think, pray, rest or prepare. Maybe it is a gift from a sender who wants you to turn your heart back to Him because it is so packed with a busy schedule and chiming voicemail that you can hardly hear His voice anymore.

Maybe waiting really is a gift. Do you disagree? Just *wait* a minute. No, really.

Provoking Thought

When you are made to wait today, as you probably will be, how can you fill that time in a way that responds to David's words, "wait for the Lord"?

A Prayer for Reflection

You keep us waiting.
You, the God of all time,
Want us to wait
For the right time in which to discover
Who we are, where we must go,
Who will be with us, and what we must do.
So, thank you... for the waiting time.

— A prayer of *The Iona Community*

Being Sure of What We Do Not See

"Now faith is the assurance of things hoped for, the conviction of things not seen."

— Hebrews 11:1

So much of our life is lived in the temporal—the here, now or perhaps tomorrow morning. I have to confess, I sometimes spend too much time there myself. As I write this, my wife and I are preparing to move to a home a bit closer to my office, which will make life more manageable.

But I am a bit caught up in all the business, such as financing, where the furniture will fit and what the renovation budget will look like. We humans do busy ourselves a lot that way, do we not? We spend lots of time with ambition, proper attention to our careers, 401Ks, where to send the kids to college, the *next* car or home to buy. Or perhaps we spend lots of time pondering old wounds, pains, grief and grudges of the past. Maybe some of us are just trying to stay afloat, *"How will I pay that bill?" "How can I face the person I cannot stand one more day?" "How can I undergo one more treatment?"*

Now not all of these are bad things. Many of them are worthy of our attention; most are important things to which we must tend. But they are not the only things, and more vitally, they are not the ***most*** important things.

We Christians say that the most important things are those that we cannot necessarily see or prove, but things we believe and live. Things like a belief in the power of prayer, in the necessity of holiness, the demands of love, the truths of redemption, mercy, grace and resurrection. All those things come as a gift of faith, as the Bible says, an outgrowth of being sure of things we cannot really see.

Unfortunately, like the world we can become distracted. Our faith can be important, but if it is not of the utmost importance, it begins to lose its power and purpose.

There is much superficial spirituality to be found in the world today. I remember going through the check-out line at a grocery store some time ago when I saw an issue of the magazine called *Self* (a sign of our times). I could not pass it up when I noticed it was the special "Spirituality" issue. There were several articles, most of them brief... articles on *Spiritual Workouts, The Ten Commandments for Today* and perhaps my favorite, *Spiritual Fashion.*

For some, Christianity is treated like this. Many believe it is generally a good thing. Church is a nice place to go. Some churchgoers believe that attending is something you should do because it is healthy, like a good workout or a day at the spa. So we read articles on how aromatherapy is spiritual, or we gobble up the morning talk show segment on how reading Whitman in the hot tub is spiritual. When a rap star whose lyrics are filled with profanity comes to the microphone to receive an award, he is always sure to grab the cross around his neck and "thank God," along with his producer and publicist. If we tune in, we might be tempted to think, *"My, he must be so spiritual."*

But let us be honest. While candles, music and even good wine can enhance spirituality, their depth of spirituality can equal that of eye shadow—easily applied, easily removed. When our spirituality is skin deep then it shows up so easily in our life commitments. A sporting event on the weekend takes precedence over our worship with God. A late-night party edges out the need to close our day in prayer. The demands of the working world keep us from studying the Scriptures.

Our financial commitments to the work of Christ slowly creep to the end of the list after things like the new plasma screen, a weekend in Vegas or new furniture for the guest room.

There is a little snippet from Paul's second letter to Timothy that moves every bit of shallow spirituality and cotton-candy theology to the back of the line. Here is a man who gave up everything for the Gospel—his reputation, his status, his friends and his wealth. And where do we find him? Bound in chains during the Neronian persecution, he languished in a dungeon, abandoned by most of his friends and awaiting execution. Paul was about to follow in the footsteps of all but two of Jesus' Apostles into martyrdom. I do not think that article will make it into the next "spirituality" issue of *Self.*

Paul, at this point, had lost everything temporal. He was, at the end, like all of the great early Christians, fighting against the empty vessel of the temporal world. His Gospel was not grounded in the world of touch, taste or smell.

This is why some of the last words Paul would ever write were not *"Look at where I am,"* but rather, *"Look at where I am going."* He writes, *"As for me, I am already being poured out as a libation, and the time of my departure has come. I have fought the good fight, I have finished the race, I have kept the faith."*[1] Paul writes what Jesus demanded; it is the one who gives up his life who saves it, not the other way around.

A real spirituality that is grounded in the self-sacrificial commitment to Christ pinches, pokes and probes. It constantly points out our need to come down off our high horses and humbly fall on our faces before the God of the universe, who was willing to pour out His life so that we might live. Thus, we throw off everything that gets in the way, each and every distraction. If we do not, our spirituality will be as shallow as a spring puddle and dry up with the first blistering rays of sun.

1 II Timothy 4:6-7.

If I was getting a bit caught up in the here and now, at the costly expense of forgetting that it is the unseen not the seen to which our faith calls us, then someone out there who is reading along may be in the same place. If so, let me invite you to join me in rereading a bit about Paul's life. *"As for me, I am already being poured out as a libation, and the time of my departure has come. I have fought the good fight, I have finished the race, I have kept the faith." "The faith,"* something the writer of Hebrews says we can *"be sure of but cannot see."*

Provoking Thought

Spend a moment and think on that temporal thing to which you are clinging just a bit too tightly today. How can you loosen your grip, or perhaps, let go altogether?

A Prayer for Reflection

Take, Lord, as your right, and receive as my gift, all my freedom, my memory, my mind and my will. Whatever I am and whatever I possess, you have given to me; I give it all back to you. Dispose of me, and the powers you gave me, according to your will. Give me only a love for you, and the gift of your grace; then I am rich enough, and ask for nothing more.

— St. Ignatius Loyola, d. 1556[2]

2 Counsell 204.

A Time for Everything

"For everything there is a season, and a time for every matter under heaven: a time to be born, a time to die; a time to plant, and a time to pluck up what is planted; a time to weep, and a time to laugh; a time to mourn, and a time to dance."

— Ecclesiastes 3:1-2, 4

Earlier today, I was looking out at my yard and I remembered a swing set that we had torn down shortly after we moved into this home. At least for now, we are out of the "swing set" season of life. A tiny bit of melancholy set in as I thought of the many swing sets in the many yards we have had over our quarter century of marriage.

My wife and I have lived in nearly a dozen homes, in six different states and with every move we have had to offer our "hellos" and "good-byes." If walls could talk, each home could speak of uproarious laughter and quiet tears, parental discipline and praise, parties with full rooms of guests and quiet evenings in front of the fire. Every carpet we left had the stains of morning coffee that sat with us through quiet times of prayer and study, and wine that tipped over the edge of a glass during a movie or a night with friends. Amazingly, we have had a garage sale in every home we have owned, and some good-serving, nonprofit organization usually made it by our home to remove the leftovers. Just recently, we sent away a chest of drawers my wife owned for over thirty years and a desk I have had since I was five.

Change rarely comes without difficulty, but when it comes, there is absolutely nothing we can do about it. There is something we can do in anticipation of it, which is to welcome it. We certainly could have resisted all the little (and big) changes that come with such a life, but then we would miss so much of the experience of life itself.

Sorry folks, it was not Pete Seeger who first wrote those words but the wise, and still unknown, author of Ecclesiastes. The central theme of which jumps out like a Jack in the Box—there is a time for everything.

It is just human nature that when we encounter change, there are some who are thrilled with the opportunity to begin again. Yet there are many others who worry about saying "good-bye" and do not know what the "hello" of the future might hold. I suppose that is okay. But we probably should not hold so fast to the past that we cannot, with joy and hope, embrace the good things that may come with the future.

You know, when that swing set was moved out, it left room for a horseshoe set and some small football games. Perhaps in another day, it will be a little meditation garden to sit and talk with growing children. That does not mean the swing set was not a good thing, it is just time for a different thing, a different season.

I finished up this little pondering with an afternoon run. I do not run as far as I used to, but as I wound it up, I passed one of my senior neighbors on an afternoon walk with his cane. My guess is someday I might be out walking with my cane when a young buck passes me on his afternoon run. At the end of the day, both can really be good in their own way, can they not?

The past, with all of its changes, merely opens the door to the future and each usually has its own little roller-coaster ride. As you look to what this day or tomorrow may bring, I bet they will be even better if you are willing to enjoy the ride; enjoy the season. *Turn, turn, turn* (that part IS by Seeger).

One more thing, person, if you will, that makes the ups and downs of the roller-coaster just a bit more manageable is Jesus Christ. We are told He is *"...the same yesterday and today and forever."*[1] Hang on to Him, and I would bet that any change that comes your way will be, in the end, just fine.

Provoking Thought

What change are you anticipating in the season ahead? How can you best welcome it into your life?

A Prayer for Reflection

Be present, O merciful God, and protect us through the silent hours of this night, so that we who are wearied by the changes and chances of this fleeting world may repose upon your eternal changelessness; through Jesus Christ our Lord. Amen.

— Pope Leo the Great, d. 61[2]

1 Hebrews 13:8.
2 *The Book of Common Prayer* 133.

Time Will Tell

"And not only that, but we also boast in our sufferings, knowing that suffering produces endurance, and endurance produces character, and character produces hope, and hope does not disappoint us, because God's love has been poured into our hearts through the Holy Spirit that has been given to us."

— Romans 5:3-5

"Only time will tell." That is one of those quotes that is, frankly, sometimes helpful and sometimes irritating. It was one my grandmother used to say a great deal when imploring "patience" from her grands about a wide variety of things.

But you know it is not a bad quote to tug on, particularly when one is moving through a dark period in life. In the moment, pain and suffering seem difficult, perhaps unbearable. In the long-term, things often look different and they can be interpreted differently. In the moment of childbirth, one rarely ponders the joy of parenting. While in the struggle of parenting, one rarely ponders the long view of a productive young adult. In the midst of graduate school, the budding attorney or medical student struggles mightily to become someone who can make a positive difference in the world. In the gym, weights curled and hurled rarely produce strong muscles without some pain. You get the picture.

But why on earth would pain have to be part of the recipe of human existence? Let me suggest an answer in two parts. First of all, one rarely thinks in terms of the long range. We are, too often perhaps, bound to a 24-hour clock. We tend to live minute by minute, hour by hour, day by day. An addict in a 30-day recovery program would likely prefer to be fixed overnight, but it does not work that way. We often want our prayers answered *"Now!"* and *"In my way!"* But we tend to forget that God is not bound by time. He is literally outside the limits of time. So perhaps our prayers are answered today for us, but in God's time, maybe they were answered yesterday before we prayed them! Hard to get? Unchain yourself from the clock when it comes to dealing with God's time and ours.

When you and I look up at a far-away star, astronomers tell us that depending on how many light years away that star is, we are actually seeing light from years, sometimes decades or even centuries before! That star may have long ago exploded and yet it is burning dimly in the eye of the present.

Physicist Stephen Hawking has quoted Augustine's belief that any god must exist outside of time. The theory of relativity has been proven with experiments that show time is not bound by our clock. For instance, if an astronaut could travel at the speed of light, as he approached that point, time would actually slow down for that person.

So an astronaut who lifts off from earth and then approaches the speed of light would return younger than someone of the same age they left back on earth! Again, it is hard to understand because we are so bound by time. But let me encourage you to let go of that notion for a moment. If you realize God works outside of our calendar, perhaps it is easier to consider that our momentary pains might be doing something good that we cannot now imagine—which leads me to the second part of my recipe.

The best way I know to sum this up is found in the passage from Romans on the first page of this meditation. It tells us that there is something about the tether connecting the passage of time with our pain that makes us more than we thought we could be. I would love to say it is easier than that, but let that explanation settle in just a moment. If you have experienced the pain of childbirth, would you give up that pain if it also meant giving up your child? If you have experienced the trials of maintaining a strong friendship or marriage, would you let go of that pain if it meant a life of loneliness? If you have experienced a measure of inner peace after a long period on your knees, would you give up that peace? If you are one who does know what it means to have a relationship with our Lord, you also know you must continue to give up, surrender your own life into His hands. Would you pass up that life for keeping yourself to yourself?

You know the words "no pain, no gain." Sounds really nifty at the gym, but it is not as much fun when you are moving through the personal pain of a struggling marriage, another chemo treatment, an estranged relationship with a child, a divided community of faith and so on. But there is truth to that bumper sticker philosophy.

Aleksandr Solzhenitsyn wrote of his own experience with the trials of pain over time, *"It was only when I lay there on rotting prison straw that I sensed within myself the first stirrings of good. Gradually, it was disclosed to me that the line separating good and evil passes, not through states, nor between classes, nor between political parties either—but right through all human hearts... So, bless you, prison, for having been in my life."*[1]

Solzhenitsyn's quote responds to both pieces of my recipe. It was not in the moment, but in looking at the "whole" of the moment, that a greater understanding about human nature and relationship to God became clearer and made sense to him. While he might have liked to have come to this realization in a different way, it was the suffering in prison that brought about that clarity.

I do not know what suffering you, who are reading this now, may be going through at this very moment, but I can tell you this, as Corrie Ten Boom wrote, *"[T]here is no pit so deep that He is not deeper still."*[2]

In my own moments of anguish it was not until it was all over that clarity, meaning and perhaps even purpose became known; it was not until much later that I could even see God's hand.

1 Aleksandr I. Solzhenitsyn, *The Gulag Archipelago 1918-1956* (New York: Harper Perennial Modern Classics, 2002) 312-313.

2 Corrie Ten Boom, *The Hiding Place* (Grand Rapids: Chosen Books, 2007) 227.

I cannot say that every mystery around pain and suffering has yet to be revealed in my own journey—there are still lots of question marks out there for me. I bet there are some for you as well. As to those, I guess my grandmother's words still are true, *"Only time will tell."*

Provoking Thought

If you are experiencing some pain in your life right now, take some time to reflect on how that pain, over time, may strengthen you more than you are now. Is there anything good that has come out of this time of pain?

A Prayer for Reflection

O God, as I travel through this pain, this trial, this struggle, be present, be present, O my strength and salvation. I pray for the end of this season of suffering that accords with Your purpose and refinement of my soul. If that pain ends now, give me a grateful heart for its relief and whatever has been gained. If its end is beyond my time of yearning, then give me power to endure, character to receive and hope to carry me to its perfect end. Amen.

— RJL+

Taste and See

"O taste and see that the Lord is good..."

— Psalm 34:8

Not too long ago, work called me away from a televised tennis match that was reaching a nail biting conclusion. Fortunately, I had a DVR, pushed the record button and went out the door. I was out rather late, and so avoided any news outlets that might have let me know the winner of the match. The next morning I woke, grabbed hold of my morning coffee, flipped on the television and hit the play button on the remote. Several times, I almost could not stand the anticipation. I was tempted just to fast-forward to see how it turned out! But something in me said *"No, you'll spoil the match if you reveal the winner too early!"*

I would bet many of us would really like a fast-forward button in our lives. When the doctor calls with the bad news, many of us would love to fast-forward to see how it all really turns out. When the boss gives the bad review, the police station calls with the news they have one of yours in custody, the market takes a turn for the worse or there is an envelope with a legal office return address! How many of us would love to just fast-forward to see how it turns out. That does not just go for bad news, but good news as well. When the tax return envelope comes, the child graduates, you meet someone who may just be that "special" someone, the boss calls offering a promotion; these too make us want to fast forward!

But if we hit the fast-forward button too much, whether in anticipation of bad news or good, then we often miss the adventure in-between. And believe it or not, there is often adventure in that "in-betweenness" of waiting for the end of the story.

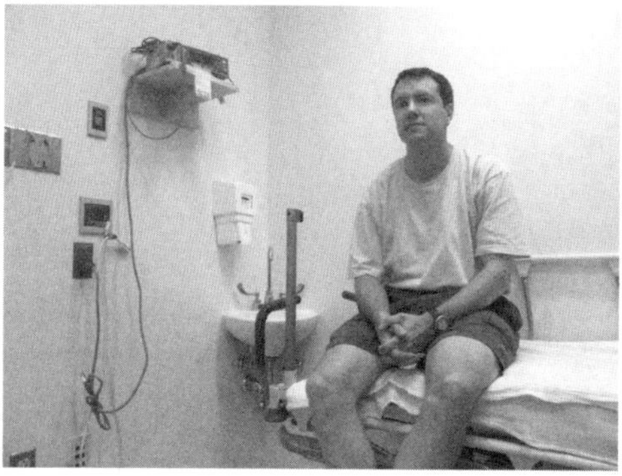

In the world in which you and I travel, so much seems to get lost in the rush of all the "busy-ness" that seems to wait patiently for each pause. We tend, in all this rushing about, to forget to hit a much more important button than fast-forward... the pause button.

I do not believe our good Lord gave us our lives to speed up so that we miss the enjoyment of the ride. When I was young, my father and I often frequented a barbeque spot in my native city of Birmingham, Alabama. The owner had posted the above verse, *"Taste and see,"* on a large plaque over his smoking BBQ pits so that all could see when they entered. As a Christian man, it was his way of reminding his patrons that the gift of food is not to be wolfed down, but instead eaten slowly, savored, enjoyed. God's gifts of our senses are also a reminder to enjoy!

I once saw a brief, one-woman play entitled *The Golden Egg*. It begins with a little girl who is frustrated with a situation at school, and she just wishes that she could go on to the next grade. An old mystic appears and gives her a golden egg with a small piece of string hanging out. The mystic tells the little girl that any time she runs into a painful, uncomfortable situation, she can pull on the string and time will fly.

In no time, the little girl snatches out a section of string and finds herself in the next grade! But moving forward faster and faster is too much of a temptation. Every time she runs into something she does not like, she yanks on that string, and sometimes she pulls too hard. So, not wanting to wait for her wedding, she gives it a yank, but then she misses the honeymoon. When the labor pains came, another yank, but then she misses the first smile and step. When her husband becomes ill she cannot take it and pulls that string. When the time passes, she misses his death and is just standing at his grave. She finally realizes what she has done and tries to back up by sticking the string back into the egg. But she cannot, and time really has flown.

Each and every day is precious, as are the moments and the relationships given to us as part of Jesus' gift of life. Players, choose not to leave the game early. Enjoy the extra time, hold hands just a bit longer, cuddle just a bit more, maybe watch the credits or sleep a little later. Perhaps turn off the smart phone and hit the pause button every chance you get. And if not the pause button, then at least the play button. For goodness sake, stay clear of the fast-forward!

Why? Taste and see! Taste and see!

Provoking Thought

How might you consciously hit the pause button this day? Why not give it a try?

A Prayer for Reflection

Lord, I have time
I have plenty of time,
All the time that you give me,
The years of my life,
The days of my years,
The hours of my days,
They are all mine.
Mine to fill, quietly, calmly,
But to fill completely, up to the brim,
To offer them to you, that of their insipid water
You may make a rich wine
such as you made once in Cana of Galilee.

— Michel Quoist[1]

1 Michel Quoist, *Prayers of Life* (Dublin: Gill & Macmillan, 1963).

Look at the Birds

"Look at the birds of the air; they neither sow nor reap nor gather into barns, and yet your heavenly Father feeds them. Are you not of more value than they?"

— Matthew 6:26

"Let the little birds be your theologians" is a thought attributed to Martin Luther. Not a bad suggestion. In His sermon on the mount Jesus said, *"Look at the birds of the air."*

I have learned a lot from birds over the years. I once considered a vocation in ornithology, but preferred people over our feathered friends. However, I am still a novice bird watcher. We have feeders in our little backyard that attract a wide array of birds—blue jays, sparrows, finches, blackbirds, cowbirds, doves of a few varieties and two of the three predominant woodpeckers in the area of Texas where I live.

The other day, I saw something I have never seen in all my years of "looking at the birds of the air." You probably know the sound a baby bird makes when it is following its mama bird about, waiting for food. A high pitched squeak comes out of the stretched open beak.

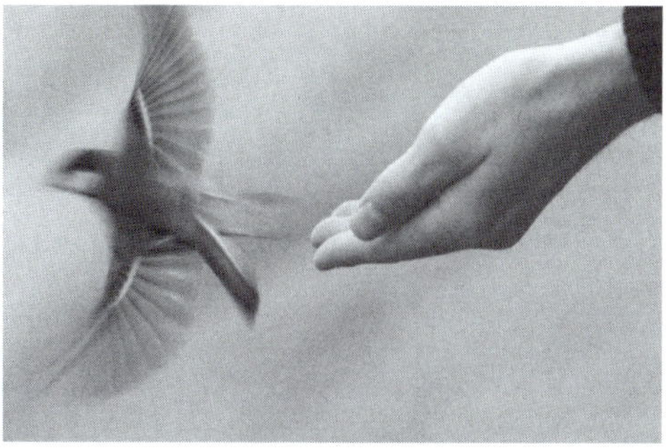

The baby often bounces and flutters its wings until the mom places a worm, piece of seed or scrap of bread into the hungry mouth. If it is a really hungry bird, this can go on for an hour or more and the sound can get a bit on the nerves!

On this particular day, I heard that squeaking outside of my bedroom window for some time and finally decided to take a peek. Much to my surprise, I found a small, brown cowbird hopping behind a bright red, *male cardinal!* Somewhere, something got turned around. This baby was *not* following around its mama, but it was following around another bird's papa—and not even of the same species! So, I was fascinated to see what the male bird would do because that babe was not letting up. It was bouncing around right on the heels of this adopted dad. Then to my surprise, the pop picked up a bit of food and went and delivered it right into the beak of his adopted child! Not once but at least twice that I saw.

Now, this goes against what we may know as the paternal nature of animals, but in reality, it is not that unusual for one bird to take another into its care. However, I have never seen it with my own eyes. And it made me think, *"I wonder if I am that attentive to the open mouths I may pass by every day?"*

We all know our expected responsibilities—parents care for children, friends care for friends or work colleagues support and encourage one another. What about being especially attentive to those in need around us, even when we are not, by nature or habit, driven or drawn to care for them? Are we really aware of the "open beaks" we encounter every day? Do we realize that the good Lord may have allowed that one to cross our path because He knows we have it in us to care for them? And do we then, in turn, do what our Lord hopes we will do?

Jesus suggested caring for others was one way of reaching out to Him, *"...just as you did it to one of the least of these who are members of my family, you did it to me."*[1] Sometimes that means visiting the sick, feeding the hungry and clothing the naked. Sometimes it may mean just being a bit kinder to that checkout lady, the bag boy, the gas station attendant or the person in traffic. Maybe it is as simple as a

1 Matthew 25:40.

smile or as intense as a visit to the ICU. I do know there are lots of little birds out there who may be waiting for you, right now, to step outside of what is expected and care when there is no one else who can.

So, let the little birds be your theologians. If a cardinal can care for one that is not his own, surely we can do the same. If only we have eyes to see Jesus was right, *"Look at the birds..."*

Provoking Thought

Watch today and tomorrow. See if there is someone in your path who needs something only you can give. Watch.

A Prayer for Reflection

Make us true servants to all those in need,
Filled with compassion in thought, word and deed;
Loving our neighbor, whatever the cost,
Feeding the hungry and finding the lost.

Lord, make us healers of body and mind;
Give us your power to bring sight to the blind;
Love to the loveless and gladness for pain,
Filling all hearts with the joy of your name.

— Susan G. Wente[2]

2 From the song, *Make Us True Servants.*

Pure Religion

"Religion that is pure and undefiled before God, the Father, is this: to care for orphans and widows in their distress, and to keep oneself unstained by the world."

—James 1:27

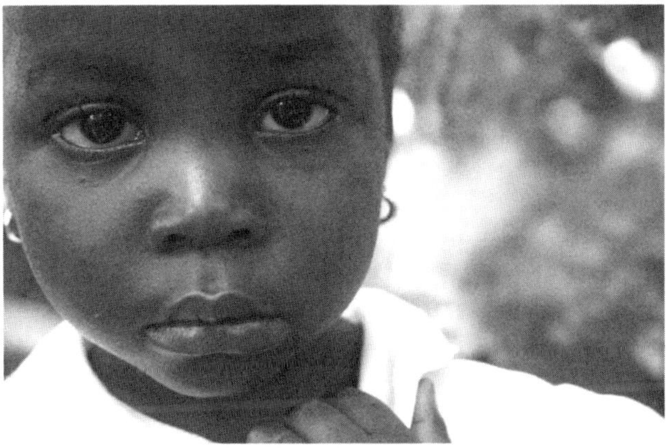

Every now and then, someone asks me to "sum up" Christianity. That is no small order, but I can cite verses like this to help me point the way. James was writing to the early Christian community who had gotten just a bit too heavy on the "faith" side of things, without living out their faith in the practice of loving deeds. Evidently those in James' particular audience had forgotten some of the orphans and widows in their care. They had gotten too caught up in faith, such that they did not mind being "stained by the world," which had about as many opportunities to be corrupt as our own.

One of the earliest heresies of the Church was called "Gnosticism." Now I could write pages, even volumes on this heresy, but one key element was the belief that somehow there was no real connection between one's soul and one's body. Thus, you could "believe" as a follower of Christ, but your body was so corrupt that it could not possibly be expected to be good. It was easy, then, for Gnostics to (a) move into Christian communities because they did share many beliefs of the early Christian communities, but then (b) become somewhat bipartisan when it came to living out their faith in deeds.

That is why James smacks them upside the head (one of my favorite Southern expressions by the way) with a reality check. *"Hey! Don't forget, pure religion is a matter of the head and the heart, faith and deeds. So don't be so heavenly good that you are no earthly good. Don't have your head in the clouds and your body in the brothel."* I could go on, but you get the point!

James' clear directive is a general reflection of Jesus' primary command that the essence of our faith is "love of God and love of neighbor."[1] It is the giving of ourselves to God in Christ through confession and repentance of sin, a total offering of ourselves to the forgiveness offered by Jesus' death on the Cross and His rising to life again. The end result of this process is a total conversion of the individual. It is living out that conversion by a consistent pattern of confession, repentance, renewal and conversion such that we begin to share the Gospel through evangelism, bringing others to Jesus Christ, and through loving deeds as found in the care of others, charity, social justice and societal change.

Thus, pure religion is a "combo meal" of committing ourselves to care for others and committing ourselves to God in Christ. For James that meant (a) caring for widows and orphans and (b) keeping oneself from being defiled by the world.

I think that is a fairly good pointer toward the essence of the faith. It would be easy to get so lost in our Christian duties that we forget we are also called to be faithful in living moral lives. I have seen many a Christian worker who has forgotten that part of the call to the Christian life—a call to goodness, purity and morality. I once had a good friend who oversaw a shelter for the community. He was doing wonderful work. I later learned that when it came to ethical practices in the business of his shelter, his record was deplorable. He seemed to think that because he was doing good in the community, it really did not matter what his means were. The end result was the total collapse of his ministry.

1 Matthew 22:37.

I have also seen those who became so caught up in keeping pure from the stains of the world that they refused to interact with those they deemed just a bit too stained to endure. How does that measure up with a Lord and Savior who spent some of His best work among prostitutes, winebibbers, tax collectors and sinners? It does not.

No, the answer is to walk both lines—caring and personal holiness. These are hard lines to walk. We all stumble, but that is why some lines are drawn to help show us the way. Getting sidetracked? Why not read James' words once more, *"Religion that is pure and undefiled before God, the Father, is this: to care for orphans and widows in their distress, and to keep oneself unstained by the world."* Better yet, read Jesus' words as you find them in Matthew 22:37. I would really like you to look it up! And then, when you do, get to it.

Provoking Thought

As James places this mark of finding a way to walk faithfully between faith and deeds before you, how does it challenge you to step more deeply in your faith? To act more faithfully in your deeds?

A Prayer for Reflection

Almighty God, in whom we live and move and have our being, you have made us for yourself, so that our hearts are restless till they rest in you; grant us purity of heart and strength of purpose, that no passion may hinder us from knowing your will, no weakness from doing it; but in your light may we see light clearly, and in your service find perfect freedom; through Jesus Christ our Lord, Amen.

— St. Augustine, d. 430[2]

2 Counsell 30.

God's Tattoo

"...when Israel sought for rest, the Lord appeared to him from far away, 'I have loved you with an everlasting love; therefore I have continued my faithfulness to you.'"

—Jeremiah 31:2-3

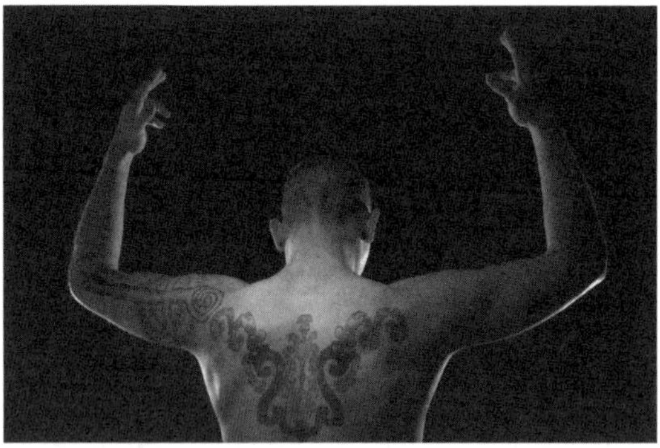

There are many things that have changed in my over half-century of life, and one of those things is the tattoo. When I was a kid, if you got a tattoo which, by the way, was taboo in my home, you ***really*** stood out of the crowd. Some sailors and military men got tattoos, but RARE was the occasion that a youth or teen followed their lead.

Well, a visit to the beach this summer and my bi-weekly trips to the gym tell me that if you ***really*** want to stand out from the crowd now, perhaps you ought *not* to get a tattoo!

I am not anti-tattoo, but I do think it is getting a bit silly. I loved a little cartoon I saw not too long ago, showing a young teen getting what she thought was a "hip" tattoo band around her bicep. The next frame showed her years later as a grandmother, with the band now down to her wrist. Then her grandchild says, *"Gee grandma, you are really cool!"* at which point the grandma rolled her eyes.

At our home, we recently heard the story of a man who had the name of his wife tattooed within a heart-shaped design on his chest.

As children came along, he began putting their names in as well. At the birth of the last, the tattoo artist actually got the name wrong—something the man did not notice until it was all over. So, what to do? They changed the name of the child to match the mistake!

I wonder if you have ever read about God's tattoo. From Holy Scripture, it tells us He only has one. It is one of the many places in the book of Isaiah where he is describing God's love for His children and it goes like this, *"I will not forget you. See, I have inscribed you on the palms of my hands..."*[1] Another version says, *"I have **engraved** you on the palm of my hand."*

Can you see that? Though metaphor for sure, can you see that as God sees that? He looks into His hand, and there is YOUR NAME. You are constantly part of God's thinking. His love is unwaning, secure and endless. He does not have your name wrong or your face wrong. He loves the one right there on His hand. You.

The passage from Jeremiah above is a bit different from much of

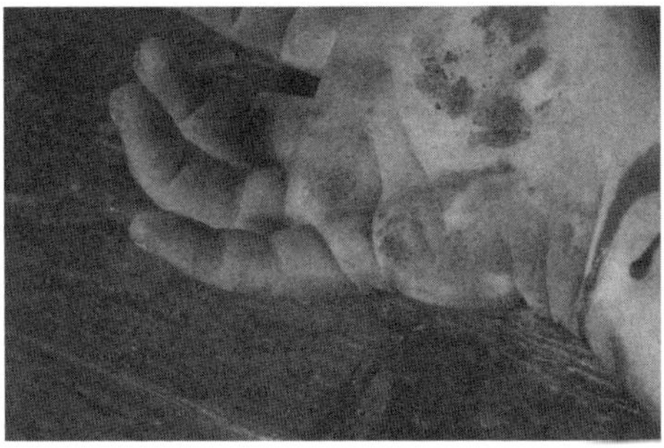

the rest of his work. For most of his writing, Jeremiah was all about doom and gloom. But in this passage, he allows those clouds to disperse just a bit, and God tells Israel that He loves them with an everlasting love. The Hebrew word was *hesed* and it means "steadfast." In other words, there is nothing in heaven or on earth that can take God's love away from you. A constant, biding, immortal love... this is what God has for you.

You know, even on the Cross, Jesus followed His heavenly Father's lead and your name was "engraved" on His hands. These same hands of love welcomed rugged iron nails to say that His love for you was more precious to Him than any other chapter of the story we know as the "universe."

God's tattoo had but one motive—love. May you rest, this day, in the security of that love.

1 Isaiah 49:16.

Provoking Thought

God's love for you is higher and deeper than any love you have ever experienced. How does resting in that knowledge change the way you will face the day ahead?

A Prayer for Reflection

Everlasting Father, You tell me that You love me with an everlasting, steadfast, immortal love—that my name is written on the palm of Your mighty hand. Free me, I pray, from the chatter of noises that rob me of the experience of that love—my own doubt and fear, anxieties and worries, inadequacy and insecurity. Help me to hear, once again, the whisper of Your unbounded love for me, that in the security of that love, I may, in return, love You and all You send my way. Amen.

— RJL+

Abundant Life

"I came that they may have life, and have it abundantly."

—John 10:10

There is a story of a young Frank Lloyd Wright out walking in the snow one day with his father. They had traveled a bit in a rural area, when his father stopped him and said, *"Frank, turn around and look at our footsteps. Do you see yours? They go from one place to another—to the bush, then the fence, here and there. Do you see mine? A straight line! And that, Frank, is how to get through this life. Keep your eyes focused on what you want to do, and you will get to where you are going!"*

On that day, Wright was said to have made a crucial promise to himself. He promised that he would never let his goals sidetrack him from enjoying life to the fullest. He wanted to be the kind of person who took time to look at the bushes and the farm animals, and to smell the roses. While still on the journey, he did not want to miss the scenery.

I think that is one of the things Jesus meant when He shared these words. The "life" in the promise here is a gift Jesus really *wants* to give us. Now what Jesus is talking about in this passage is not the gift of resurrected or eternal life. Nor is He saying what some foolish religious leaders promise—follow Jesus and everything you do will flourish and prosper

(a terrible falsehood found nowhere in the Holy Scriptures). No, what He is trying to do is to remind His followers that each moment of life is a precious treasure.

It is so easy in this world to be burdened by daily responsibilities; we all have them. There are, and always will be, so many tasks that go into fulfilling our goals of health, security or professional success. Why not consider committing to making certain that your goals will not sidetrack you from enjoying the life we have been given?

Where to start? Just a few suggestions: spend some time watching a movie with a friend, spouse, child or, better yet, spend a bit more time talking together. Stop a few times a day, take a deep breath and look out your window. Pray a bit more. Listen a bit more. Read a bit more. Or perhaps just *stop* a bit more.

Here is a list of things that will *always* be waiting for you: bills, the yard, phone calls, e-mails, the mail, your mortgage company, landlords, your insurance bills and many more. I am not suggesting they be ignored. They have to be tended to, just not *all* the time.

Here are some things that may *not* always be around: your child's story from school today, a rose that has just opened, a meal with a friend at a new restaurant, the first glass of wine from a new bottle, the first morning cup of coffee, your wife reaching out to hold your hand, your mother who called "just to talk," your father who wants to pitch the ball or watch the game. You could miss new insights from reading the Holy Scriptures before you start your day, and the voice you might hear or direction you may receive if you spend just a few minutes in the morning or before bed, in prayer. You get the picture.

Abundant life is really a very good gift if we receive it. Let us follow Frank Lloyd around a bit and we may see something we might have missed!

Provoking Thought

What would happen if you simply pushed aside the mail, turned off your phone and computer and had just a bit more silence in the day ahead?

A Prayer for Reflection

Almighty God, still now, my rapid pace. Ease my racing heart, still my racing mind, stop my racing feet. Give me eyes to see, ears to hear, and fingers to touch the abundant life springing up all around me. Help me to find joy in this gift You have given me, and to take each moment as a precious jewel from Your hand into mine. Amen.

— RJL+

Reality Check

"The heavens are telling the glory of God; And the firmament proclaims his handiwork. Day to day pours forth speech, And night to night declares knowledge. There is no speech, nor are there words; their voice is not heard; yet their voice goes out through all the earth, and their words to the end of the world."

— Psalm 19:1-4

While I was away on vacation not too long ago, the priest at a small parish that rests on the north Atlantic coastline of Maine decided to hold worship outdoors. The chairs faced our Lord's Table with a background of rushing waves smashing into the rugged boulders and layers of prehistoric rocks jutting out of the sands below. The sky, gently pocked with wisps of fluffy clouds, was a particular blue that no painter's brush could match. Gulls dove for unseen fish and black cormorants stood motionless, holding out their wings to embrace the brisk winds.

I certainly participated in the worship by listening to the lessons and sermon, singing the songs, praying the prayers and consuming the Lord's Supper. While I did all of these things, a portion from the opening Scripture popped into my head, *"The heavens are telling the glory of God."*

"The heavens tell." No spoken or written words, no movie or play, no art or music but the heavens themselves *speak* of God's majesty, handiwork, presence and His being.

We all know the two words "reality check." It is usually a sarcastic metaphor for a kind of slap in the face that says, *"Hey! Wake up and pay attention, this is important!"* Sometimes that comes in the form of a bill stamped "Overdue," or a mortgage statement that reads "Final Notice." Sometimes the reality check is a coach or teacher raising their voice, calling our name, issuing the words, *"Listen up!"* Sometimes it is the doctor who comes in tapping the clipboard and saying *"We've got to talk,"* or the spouse who flips off the television and says, *"You are not listening."* A reality check usually gets us back on some track we are supposed to be traveling and off of which we have stumbled.

There are a number of reality checks in nature too: the chameleon that takes time to sun itself on a rock; the pup that delights in playing fetch; the mother hen embracing chicks under her wings; the oak tree with deep roots that last for centuries; the pecan tree with its shallow roots that topples when the ground is too wet; the anemone and clown fish, or shark and remora that live with one another though completely different; the lioness who feasts with abandon or the hyena that laughs with its mates; the sparks in a friend's eyes; the unclothed skin of your loved one with smooth and rolling landscapes of textures and shades; the stars that burn without apology and the rising and setting sun that remind us of their constant presence.

It would be easy to ignore the reality check nature offers us. There is so much stuff that we humans make to tell our story. But then, that story is really just a kind of chapter when held up against the stage of God's majestic epic.

Don't see Him? Look up, look around, just look.

Provoking Thought

Sometime today, God will likely surprise you with some lesson from the world He has created, if you just take time to look. Open your eyes. See if you can agree that the heavens are sending a little reality check that reminds you of the Glory of God.

A Prayer for Reflection

I praised the earth, in beauty seen
With garlands gay of various green;
I praised the sea, whose ample field
Shone glorious as a silver shield;
And earth and ocean seemed to say
'Our beauties are but for a day!'

I praised the sun, whose chariot rolled
On wheels of amber and of gold;
I praised the moon, whose softer eye
Gleamed sweetly through the summer sky,
And moon and sun in answer said,
'Our days of light are numbered!'

O God! O good beyond compare!
If thus thy meaner works are fair;
If thus thy bounties gild the span
Of ruined earth and sinful man;
How glorious must the mansion be
Where thy redeemed shall dwell with thee!

— Reginald Heber, d. 1826
A Bishop of Calcutta[1]

1 Counsell 355.

Serving Marvelously

"For we are what He has made us, created in Christ Jesus for good works, which God prepared beforehand to be our way of life."

— Ephesians 2:10

"A domino factum est illud, et est mirable in oculis meis!" When news reached Elizabeth that she would be the new reigning monarch of England upon the death of her sister Mary, these were the words she was heard to say. Translation, *"This is the doing of the Lord and it is marvelous in our eyes."*[1]

When one reads the history of Queen Elizabeth I, one of the things that seems so evident is that all of her life, Elizabeth was prepared for her role as one of the most significant and influential monarchs in the history of the United Kingdom. Her gifts and the needs of her country were a perfect fit for the season of her leadership.

If you are an adult much beyond the age of twenty-five, then you probably have witnessed a funeral for a well-known political figure, be it a president or prime minister, senator, governor, civic leader or religious

1 Psalm 118:23.

figure. When death occurs, mourning and thanksgiving begin, and those of good character seem to be able to rise to the occasion and praise the changes such a leader has made throughout his work in the world.

One of the underlying principles of Christianity is that you and I were put on this earth to *do* something. But Christianity also teaches us that you do not have to be the Queen of England, a governor, a bank president or movie celebrity to do something important.

Christianity says that when we respond to work that God asks us to do, that is living out our calling. There are certainly some *big* jobs in the world's eyes, but whatever you are called to do with your life, if you are living into your calling it is *big* in God's eyes. That goes for stay-at-home moms and dads, for garbage collectors, pool cleaners and, yes, for CEOs and rock stars. This is why Paul writes the words above to the Christians scattered throughout the region of Ephesus. Perhaps a modern translation of Paul's words might be, *"Don't forget! You were created by God for a purpose! To do good things! To carry out good work! That's the way we are supposed to live!"*

From time to time it is good to revisit one's calling. *"Why am I doing what I am doing? Am I living into my call as fully as I could? What needs to be added in, cut out or changed?"*

Frederick Buechner has some good words for us here:

> *Vocation... It comes from the Latin "vocare," to call, and means the work a man is called to do by God. There are different kinds of voices calling you to all different kinds of work, and the problem is to find out which is the voice of God rather than of Society, or the Superego, or Self-Interest. By and large a good rule for finding out is this. The kind of work God usually calls you to is the kind of work (a) that you need most to do and (b) that the world most needs to have done. If you really get a kick out of your work, you've presumably met (a), but if your work is writing TV deodorant commercials, the chances are you've missed requirement (b). On the other hand, if your work is being a doctor in a leper*

> *colony, you have probably met requirement (b), but if most of the time you're bored or depressed by it, the chances are you have not only bypassed (a) but probably aren't helping your patients much either. Neither the hair shirt nor the soft berth will do. The place God calls you to is the place where your deep gladness and the world's hunger meet.*[2]

Perhaps it is time to spend a few ticks of the clock to reflect on what you are doing with your life. Can you say of your vocation *"A domino factum est illud, et est mirable in oculis meis"*?

If not, then perhaps begin to pray about what would be "marvelous in His eyes," and yours. But if you have found your calling, then do not forget to give thanks for the marvelous gift of vocation—a calling that is only yours and a need in the world that can only be met by you.

Provoking Thought

Are you living into your vocation? Why did you choose to "do" what you are doing? Is it a match between your gifts and the world's needs? Is it time for a change or time simply to pause and give thanks?

A Prayer for Reflection

O send thy light and thy truth, that we may live always near to thee, our God. Let us feel thy love, that we may be as it were already in heaven, that we may do all our work as the angels do theirs. Let us be ready for every work, be ready to go out or come in, to stay or to depart, just as thou shalt appoint. Lord, let us have no will of our own, or consider our true happiness as depending in the slightest degree on anything that can befall us outwardly, but as consisting altogether in conformity to thy will; through Jesus Christ our Lord. Amen.

— Henry Martyn, d. 1812
A missionary and priest[3]

2 Buechner 95.
3 Counsell 354.

The One Who's Got Your Back

"The Lord is my rock, my fortress, and my deliverer, my God, my rock, in whom I take refuge, my shield and the horn of my salvation, my stronghold and my refuge, my savior; you save me from violence. I call upon the Lord, who is worthy to be praised, and I am saved from my enemies."

— II Samuel 22:2-4

Protection. The word alone brings both a sense of comfort, and perhaps heightened anxiety. We all want protection, and the thought of not having it brings a sense of angst, as if there is no covering, no footing, no "refuge" as David says above.

I have been fortunate to meet and spend time with three former Presidents. The first time this occurred, I had to go through not hours, but days of screening and background checks. In subsequent meetings, whether while attending a meeting or riding in a motorcade, the security seemed to be on every side. Windows were bulletproof; Secret Service agents were ubiquitous. Firearms were either hidden, or at times out in the open. There is no question that such security, particularly in today's world, is necessary. No question that there are those who, in the words well known to most teens, had the President's "back." And to be honest, on those occasions I, too, was grateful for the added security—the "refuge."

But few of us have that kind of protection. And even if we did, it does not protect from everything, like illness and disease. Even still, I would bet most of us would like it.

My college roommate introduced me to a spray-on coating that when applied to the dashboard, leather or vinyl seating, the steering wheel and even auto tires, can make a car look almost new in an instant. This spray-on "armor" gave you the impression that the material underneath was protected from the external elements. But, of course, within a few days the coating would thin and the dinks would show up.

Who has got *your* back? Is there a kind of armor coating you can find to protect you from the slings and arrows of this world? A full bank account can provide job security, a large home, the right car, perhaps even the right reputation or friends. While some of these may enhance our "abundant life," (see page 51) ultimately they do not provide a real refuge.

When David wrote the words here he was, in a sense, besieged not only with real enemies, but also with a multitude of personal problems. What we see here is that he did not turn to armor, weapons, wealth, or the ancient Secret Service! He knew that when the going really got tough, God had his back.

There are, of course, measures we should all take to protect ourselves from physical harm that could befall anyone—an alarm system, airport security, eating right and putting on your seatbelt. But these are not refuges that can ultimately give us salvation.

When Jerusalem was so far from the place that God wanted that holy city to be, Jesus took pity on her and said, *"How often have I desired to gather your children together as a hen gathers her brood under her wings."*[1] It was Jesus' way of saying He wanted to protect those children. He wanted them to know He had their back. He did, He does and He has yours too.

1 Luke 13:34.

It is not that God was not looking out for David; He was. It was not that Jesus was not looking out for Jerusalem; He was. The Secret Service is always looking out for the President—whether he is awake or asleep; whether he is attentive to the protection or not, they are always there.

David's prayer was not so much a plea as it was a personal reminder to be in touch with the one who had his back and has yours.

Provoking Thought

When do you find yourself most fearful? What comfort is there for you in knowing that God "has your back"?

A Prayer for Reflection

May Jesus go before us to guide us;
Be beneath us to secure us;
Be behind us to protect us;
Be above us to watch over us;
And be beside us to befriend and bless us;
All the days of our life. Amen.

— The Reverend Dr. John Claypoool, d. 2005

Who Is On Your Throne?

"...He is Lord of lords and King of kings, and those with Him are called and chosen and faithful."

— Revelation 17:14

One of the astounding claims about Jesus of Nazareth was that when it came to authority, the buck stopped with Him. The passage above is a piece of the apocalyptic visions of the end of time when evil will finally be vanquished. During Jesus' life, calling Him "king" was cause for praise by some and condemnation by others.[1]

Christians today often refer to Jesus as their king. Such kingship is probably not easily lived out in our day-to-day lives; there are likely many things vying for the throne of our hearts. Calling Jesus king gives us the opportunity to stop and consider who or what really is the center of our lives—who or what "is boss" so to speak. In the United States it is very uncommon for any of us to fully understand what it would mean to have a monarch, though much more common in the United Kingdom or other parts of the world. In a worldly sense, a monarch is to be followed and obeyed, without reservation or question, because it is hoped, that at the end of the day, the monarch knows what is best for the land. We know the frailty of humanity has produced no perfect monarchs. But there is one who has walked the earth.

Jesus speaks much of "His Kingdom," and He says it is not of this world.[2] Jesus was constantly giving us glimpses into that kingdom through His teachings, actions, healings, through His death, resurrection and ascension.

If we choose to follow this king named Jesus, it will have tremendous applications in our personal lives. It will mean when we are forced or

1 Luke 19:38; Matthew 27:11.
2 John 18:33-37.

invited to take a stand for Jesus, then what we decide to do will reveal the kingdom to which we belong. Let me give you a good example.

A few years back, it was reported that a *British Airways* ticket agent was told by a supervisor to take off the small cross she was wearing. She decided to take voluntary leave rather than remove the cross. Once it hit the wider news, a furor began. Everyone from political action committees to the Archbishop of York had an opinion.

Now we all know that plenty of people wear crosses, many of whom have no authentic or real allegiance to Christ or a life of Christian discipleship. But then again, many wear it for precisely that reason.

A friend of mine who is an editor and writer, David Kalvelage, reflected on this little cultural battle. After the dust settled, he wrote:

> *A cross is the most identifiable symbol of being a Christian… Christians who wear a cross show others that they embrace the Christian way of life. The cross is also a sign of Christ's suffering and his eternal victory over death. Those who wear it should be willing to take up their cross and follow him. The woman who refused to remove it witnessed to her faith more effectively than most of us will ever do.*[3]

Perhaps every single day, most of us have not one chance, but multiple opportunities to declare our allegiance to our King. Whether that is a moment under public display, or in the private corners of your life, how you respond will tell you who or what calls the shots in your life.

Before you make your choice, remember we Christians believe that our creation, redemption and purpose spring to life from Christ and His Kingdom. The same One who created you also knows the secrets of joy and the perfect way to live your life. Why then would any of us ever choose any other king but Christ?

3 David Kalvelage, *The Living Church* (19 Nov. 2006) 11.

Provoking Thought

See your heart as a throne. Who or what is sitting on that throne as your king?"

A Prayer for Reflection

O Lord; O King, resplendent on the citadel of heaven,
All hail continually;
And of your clemency upon your people still have mercy.
Lord, whom the hosts of cherubim in songs and hymns
With praise continually proclaim, upon us eternally have mercy.
The armies aloft, O Lord, sing high praise to you;
Those to whom the seraphim reply, 'have mercy.'
O Christ, enthroned as king above,
Whom the nine orders of angels in their beauty
        Praise without ceasing,
Upon us, your servants, ever have mercy.
O Christ, hymned by your one and only church
        Throughout the world,
To whom the sun, and moon, and stars, the land and sea,
Ever do service, have mercy.
O Christ, those holy ones, the heirs of the eternal country,
One and all with utter joy proclaim you in a most worthy strain;
Have mercy upon us.
O Lord, O gentle son of Mary free;
O King of kings, blessed redeemer;
Upon those who have been ransomed from the power of death,
By your own blood ever have mercy.
O noblest unbegotten Son, having no beginning,
Yet without effort (in the weakness of God) excelling all things,
Upon this your people in your pity, Lord have mercy.
O sun of righteousness, in all unclouded glory,
        supreme dispenser of justice,
in that great day when you strictly judge all nations,
we earnestly beseech you, upon this your people,
who here stand before your presence,
in your pity, Lord, then have mercy on us.

— Dunstan, d. 988
Archbishop of Canterbury[4]

4 Counsell 92.

One Worth Worshipping

"Then God spoke all these words:
I am the Lord your God, who brought you out of the land of Egypt, out of the house of slavery; you shall have no other gods before me."

— Exodus 20:1-3

So, what are we to make of the *American Idol* phenomenon? Season after season it is arguably one of the most successful entertainment franchises in world history. Astoundingly, in one recent season, over 50 million votes were cast for the winner. A more recent *Associated Press poll* reported that 35 percent of Americans believe votes on *Idol* matter as much as or more than those cast in a United States Presidential election!

Idolatry can be defined as the divine worship given to an image, anyone or anything but the true God. Now, I am certainly not going to be

a zealot on this one because I do watch the show! But here is the rub... idolatry, or worshipping anything other than God, is wrong—flat out, plain old, "no bones about it" wrong. A quick Sunday school memory jog will remind you that the first four of the Ten Commandments, in some way, pointed to the sin of idolatry. The first in a list usually denotes priority. There is no exception here when God says through Moses, "no other gods." Note the word "no" there. I think it hits the proverbial nail on the head.

In the last meditation, we looked a bit at paying tribute to the Divine as a king. Calling one king or queen usually has to do with matters of authority. Words like obedience, rule, perhaps even treason come to mind. But worshipping something has a bit more to do with "heart" and denoting affection, devotion or homage. A king may win our hearts, but not always. We looked at the monarch business in the last meditation; let us look for just a moment at the object of our worship.

Now what is the problem with paying a little homage elsewhere? Well, primarily, God said "no" (see previous page). Secondly, God said "no" for a good reason. God knew we humans will often run after the wrong thing to feed the hunger of our hearts and quench the thirsts of our souls. The problem with that is that anything but God will never be enough and will never, ever satisfy. I speak from personal experience here; I have tried other things. From time to time, I find those things that should not be there, slipping into that place of devotion in my heart.

There are all kinds of things that can be gods; most of them have a rather addictive quality. Success can be a god. Pleasure can be a god. A hobby can be a god. Do you remember the story of the Mt. Everest climbers who walked right past David Sharp who had collapsed from a lack of oxygen? Unwilling to stall their own ascent, dozens of people walked right past him, and he died a few hours later. Sir Edmund Hillary, who first climbed the summit in 1953, called it "horrifying" that climbers would leave a dying man.

Family can be a god, which is why, sometimes, you see a

family break apart when one or more members spin out of control. Food, rest, drink, sex, books and chocolate—the list goes on.

Now a bit of clarification. There is nothing intrinsically wrong with, let us say, money. For instance, a common misquote of the Bible is "money is the root of all evil," when the actual quote is *"the love of money is a root of all kinds of evil."*[1] There is nothing sinful, at ground zero, with watching or enjoying *American Idol*, playing golf, hunting, cross stitching or loving your children. The problem comes when that devotion, love and commitment, in any sense, "replaces" what is owed to the One who created, redeemed, saved and sustains us.

So as we consider who or what may be on the throne of our hearts, perhaps we can also consider who or what has the affection of our hearts, so much so that we are willing to worship the object of our affection? "What" may need to be chucked out of the way of that "who." Our Lord visited this planet earth for all kinds of reasons—one of which was to convict us of those things which are not right in our bodies, souls, heart and strength. Perhaps that is why Jesus said the greatest commandment was, in fact, to love God with those four aspects of our being.[2] But another reason Jesus came was to create in us clean hearts and renew our own spirits, which means that there is always the chance to begin again, if you and I are willing to turn from whatever our favorite idol is, and put the God of all creation as the primary object of our affection.[3]

So do not let your own "idol worship" be the death of you, but also do not slip into despair. The conviction that I invite you to consider here is somewhat like a doctor pointing out the infection. The difference here is I do not know what your infection is, but I will bet you do,

1 I Timothy 6:10.
2 Mark 12:30.
3 Psalm 51:10.

and I will bet God does as well. It may not be the next *American Idol*, but probably something or someone much more dangerous. The good news is that when we invite Jesus in to mend us, the health that begins to be restored will carry us through this life to the next. The One that does that for us is One worth worshipping.

Provoking Thought

What idols pull the devotion of your heart away from worshipping God? Make a list and then call on God to help you release anything that stands in the way of your pure devotion to Him.

A Prayer for Reflection

Father, as we now prepare to share in the activity of worship cleanse our hearts and minds, fill us with your Holy Spirit, and open our lips to show forth your praise; for the sake of Jesus Christ our Lord. Amen.[4]

4 Frank Coloquhoun, *Contemporary Parish Prayers* (London: Hodder & Stoughton Religious, 2005).

Help!

"'All things are lawful for me,' but not all things are beneficial. 'All things are lawful for me,' but I will not be dominated by anything."

— I Corinthians 6:12

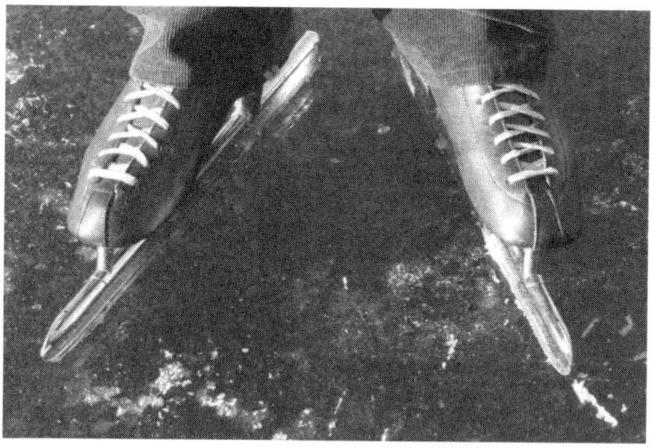

On a recent day off, I spent a bit of time exploring the city in which I now live. Clearly, there is no shortage of things to do in the greater Houston area so it is hard to know where to begin! However, needless to say, a trip to the Galleria had to be early on the agenda.

The biggest draw for our youngest was the ice skating rink. I, somewhat reluctantly, joined him on the ice. I kept thinking how I would explain an injury to my parishioners. It had been years since I gave it a whirl, but after a while I got used to the ice. While no tricks were involved, there were no spills either. How humbling to see six-year-olds speed around me on either side!

At one point, however, I was going a bit faster than expected and I am not real clear on the stopping bit. Heading full tilt toward a curve, I, with a great deal of embarrassment, slammed into the wall surprising a young mom who was keeping an eye on her kids from the sidelines. I smiled, swallowed my pride, apologized for giving her a little jolt and said, *"I've got the going part down, it's the stopping that I haven't got yet!"*

Believe it or not, my mind quickly turned to the little Scripture that the Apostle Paul uses when writing to the Church in Corinth. In these last few meditations, we have been wrestling with improper priorities (kingship, idolatry). It could be said that a real issue related to both keeping the proper king on the throne and steering clear of idols is excess. The idea is that there can be "too much of a good thing."

Too often, perhaps, we focus on the bad in the world around us so much. Paul's point was a reminder that God's real desire is for His children to enjoy life. When things go awry it is usually because we, out of ignorance, selfishness or perhaps downright rottenness, have taken something good and turned it in a way God did not intend. That is why all of this came to mind when I slammed into the wall at the "Polar Ice Rink." I think most of us have the *going* part down, it is the *stopping* part that is often hard to manage. But when we forget that, we also tend to forget there are always messy and painful consequences to our wrongful actions. I noticed some small print on my little ice skating ticket, *"...by accepting this ticket patron hereby accepts any and all inherent risk associated with ice sports..."* There is much in life that could have a similar warning label slapped on it.

God made food and a good meal is wonderful, but the intent was not gluttony. God made the pieces of a good wine, but not with the hope of drunkenness. Sexual intimacy was one of God's most wonderful gifts to humankind, not to be lived out indiscriminately or promiscuously, but within that context of marriage and fidelity. Having our basic needs met is a good thing. Even luxury can be a good thing, but kept "unchecked" it can quickly spin out of control and all kinds of ugly fruits begin to pop out—excess, selfish ambition, materialism.

The problem with many of the spoiled good things is that many of us know how to do the *going*, but it is the *stopping* with which we have trouble. How to remedy the problem? Reflection at the end of each day, spiritual direction from your clergy, the support of Christian fellowship, the gift of worship, the wealth of knowledge available through the Holy Scriptures and the way our Lord works in and through all of these things, and many more.

I suppose one chief avenue is prayer. When you see that wall approaching fast, when you feel like you've begun to breach the God-given levee, then reach out with heart and voice in prayer. *"Help!"* It is a good starting place at getting a handle not just on the *going*, but the *stopping* as well. Do you not agree?

Provoking Thought

Spend some time reflecting on an area of your life in which something may be lawful, but not beneficial. In short, where is the excess that needs to be controlled?

A Prayer for Reflection

Almighty God, Who alone can bring order to the unruly wills and passions of sinful humanity: Give your people grace so to love what you command and to desire what you promise, that, among the many changes of this world, our hearts may surely there be fixed where true joys are to be found; through Jesus Christ our Lord. Amen.[1]

1 Andrew Burnham, comp. *A Pocket Manual of Anglo-Catholic Devotion* (New York: Canterbury, 2003) 197.

Ouch

"Then Job answered the Lord: 'I know that you can do all things, and that no purpose of yours can be thwarted.' You asked, 'Who is this that hides counsel without knowledge?' Therefore I have uttered what I did not understand, things too wonderful for me, which I did not know.
'Hear, and I will speak; I will question you, and you declare to me.' I had heard of you by the hearing of the ear, but now my eye sees you; therefore I despise myself, and repent in dust and ashes."

— Job 42:1-6

"The patience of Job." That is probably something that you have either said or has been said to you at some time during your life. But if you know the rather long and depressing story of Job, you know that Job did not have patience—it ran out. As we say in my part of the country, when he had reached rope's end, he pitched a fit.

Job basically raised his hand and said, *"Hey, I don't get it! I'm a pretty good guy! I thought we had some kind of deal! I just don't understand what's up with all this suffering!"*

Have you had moments like that? I have. Suffering, pain (short or long term) is no fun. It hurts. Physical pain usually can be numbed. Not so for other kinds of pain—emotional, mental, even spiritual. Whether we walk with God or not, it may be that out of our pain, we take time to shake our fist to the sky and ask *"Why?"*

It may seem a bit simple, and perhaps not the best balm for an ailing wound. Sometimes the answer is just beyond our grasp. Sometimes when we ask God to stop the suffering He says, "no," sometimes He says, "wait," and sometimes He says, "trust Me." Sometimes we actually grow through pain and suffering. I am not promoting it and I do not think God is a sadist, but I do think often there is more to suffering than meets the eye.

Storyteller Bruce Waltke said that one day as a boy at his grandparents' country home, he was walking in the forest and he came upon something one rarely sees. It was a small chrysalis spinning around, about to break open with a new butterfly. Part of one wing broke through which was right at his eye level. He was moved by how the butterfly struggled so hard to emerge from the cocoon.

Waltke thought, *"I will just give him a little help."* So he reached down, ever so carefully and cut the top of the cocoon off with the hope of giving the butterfly a little help in its journey toward growth. Instead, the butterfly came out quickly but still very damp. It stood for a while on the edge of the cocoon and then dropped to the floor and died. He said he learned something very important that day. Sometimes we need the struggle of emergence to survive.

That is another way of saying that, sometimes in the midst of pain or suffering, we do not see what the end result may be. There is an old fable about a little piece of wood who was complaining bitterly because its owner was whittling away at it, cutting it, filling it with holes. The one who was cutting so remorselessly paid no attention to its complaining. He was making a flute out of that piece of wood and he finally said to the complaining stick, *"Little piece of wood, without these holes, and all this cutting, you would be a black stick forever—just a useless piece of ebony. What I am doing now may make you think I am destroying you, but instead, I will change you into a flute, and your sweet music will charm the souls of others and comfort many a sorrowing heart. My cutting is the making of you, for only thus can you be a blessing to the world."*[1]

After Job pitched his little fit, God responded. God began with these words, *"Who is this that darkens counsel by words without*

1 This quote was taken from personal notes kept throughout the author's ministry.

knowledge? Gird up your loins like a man. I will question you..."[2] I would not want to be on the other end of God's response.

Job's response? (See the introductory Scripture.) *"Oh, You created the universe; You created me; You have a much better view of things from where You sit. If it's okay, I'll just take all that back."*

I do not mean to make too light of suffering. Some of you reading this have suffered, and perhaps are suffering terrible things. I have as well. In the midst of some of those, I could never have known how God might have redeemed them. But in most cases, He did. And He still does.

Provoking Thought

Can you think of a time when God actually worked in your suffering? If you are suffering now, can you see God's hand at work? If not, then seek it out. If you cannot seek it out, just offer it up to Him in prayer.

A Prayer for Reflection

O Lord God, our heavenly Father, regard, we pray, with Thy divine pity the pains of all Thy children; and grant that the Passion of our Lord and His infinite love may make fruitful for good the tribulations of the innocent, the suffering of the sick, and the sorrows of the bereaved; through Him who suffered in our flesh and died for our sake, the same thy Son Jesus Christ our Lord. Amen.

— A prayer that was published and encouraged for use during World War I[3]

2 Job 38:2-3.
3 Counsell 468.

Yea! Thou Art With Me!

"The Lord is my shepherd, I shall not want. He makes me lie down in green pastures; he leads me beside still waters; he restores my soul. He leads me in right paths for his name's sake. Even though I walk through the darkest valley, I fear no evil; for you are with me..."

— Psalm 23:1-4

I spent the better part of this day preparing for a memorial service for a member of my parish. The family member with whom I met asked, as hundreds before her have, that we read Psalm 23, a portion of which is above. Perhaps the most moving line in the Psalm for those who struggle with dark valleys is that last bit, maybe better known to you in the traditional King James Version, *"Yea though I walk through the valley of the shadow of death... Thou art with me..."*

Why is that so comforting? In the last meditation we looked at suffering, but in this one, allow me to stretch it out a bit. If we "get" the lesson of suffering, can we not just "get" to the end of the valley of the shadow of death?

You will note in the last meditation, I said that sometimes God's answer to us is perhaps *"Trust me. I know what I am doing."* That really is hard, is it not? I mean we would all like a god we can control. We would probably much prefer a god who is more like the ancient genie in the lamp.

I agree with priest and writer, Barbara Brown Taylor. I really liked the story of *Aladdin* and his magic lamp. Disney did it rather well just a few years ago. The genie was funny, the bad guy lost and Aladdin learned the value of being himself.

But, as Brown Taylor points out, there is another insight that is hard for a preacher to miss—a genie is much more appealing than God.

With a genie you know you have three wishes which you can redeem whenever you like. If the genie gets on your nerves in the meantime, you can make him go back into his lamp where he can play solitaire until you need him again. ***Your*** will is his command, and if you are like me on wish number three, you wish for three more wishes!

The difference between God and a genie is clear. God is not in the business of granting wishes. God is in the business of bringing sight to the blind, wholeness to the broken and raising the dead![1]

What does that mean? It means that while we are not promised that we do not have to walk through the valley of the shadow of death, we are promised that when we do, if we are willing to receive it, God will take our hand and travel alongside us.

There is a wonderful old prayer that goes like this: *"I said to the man who stood at the gate: 'Give me a light that I may tread safely into the unknown.' And he replied: 'Go out into the darkness and put your hand into the hand of God. That shall be to you better than light and safer than a known way.'"*[2]

Few people I have met have understood this better than a young friend of mind named Emily. Emily was a Latin major at the University of the South where I served as a chaplain some years ago now.

Shortly after her birth, Emily contracted rheumatic fever and as a result, rheumatoid arthritis. When this illness strikes, it is in fact merciless and often crippling for life. Emily now stands just under five feet tall, unable to bend her legs. She used to ride a small cart around campus and had to depend on fellow classmates to carry her up stairs—an experience she and I shared on more than one occasion.

1 Barbara Brown Taylor, *Gospel Medicine* (Boston: Cowley Publications, 1995) 109-110.
2 Batchelor 146.

The growth of her arms and fingers was stunted, so holding eating utensils and carrying a meal tray were daily challenges. Over the years of her adolescence, Emily had an average of two operations every twelve months, wearing upon her body the scars of hopeful treatments. Emily is one of the most delightful people I have ever met. She never seemed embarrassed and I have never heard her complain. I long wondered the secret of her contentment.

One evening, I asked her to speak about her life to the college community. She walked her hearers through what most would describe as a lifetime of horrors. Surgery after surgery, one try after another to establish some sort of normalcy. The words that will ring in my ears for as long as I have memory were these, as she closed by saying: *"If I had my life to live over again, I wouldn't change a thing. This affliction has demanded that I walk with God daily, depend on Him constantly, for my very survival. I know He loves me as I am and I know He is the source of real life."*

This young Christian had every reason to give up on God and on life, but her commitment to Christ brought as much healing to her as if her crippled limbs were restored to wholeness. Emily did not let suffering get the best of her, and she was healed not in body, but in soul. And, for her, that is all that mattered. What I saw was not the desperate illness, but the power of God being revealed in her life.

So, when it seems like you are in that *"valley of the shadow of death,"* perhaps the best thing to grab hold of is God, and the best thing to say is *"Yea! Thou art with me!"*

Provoking Thought

Are you traveling through the valley of the shadow of death right now? Are you holding God's hand? Are you letting God hold yours? If not, perhaps start now.

A Prayer for Reflection

Lord, make possible for me by grace what is impossible to me by nature. You know that I am not able to endure very much, and that I am downcast by the slightest difficulty. Grant that for Your sake I may come to love and desire any hardship that puts me to the test, for salvation is brought to my soul when I undergo suffering and trouble for you.

— Thomas à Kempis, d. 1471[3]

3 Batchelor 165.

Trusting the Engineer

"Listen to advice and accept instruction, that you may gain wisdom for the future. The human mind may devise many plans, but it is the purpose of the Lord that will be established."

— Proverbs 19:20-21

I just got a call, which is not uncommon in my business, that a member of my parish has had an unexpected setback in recovery from a medical procedure. Now it is not critical or life-threatening. She will be fine, just not when and how she expected. She had plans to move along quicker and get back to work and play, but the plans have changed now. There is a setback, an unexpected and, frankly, unwelcome surprise. Recently, a good friend told me something that I have never spent much time thinking about. She said, *"Anger is usually the result of disappointment in unmet expectations."* There are other kinds of anger, but the more I have thought about it, the more I figure she is right. Whenever I get crossed up with someone, it is usually because they have disappointed me or, more likely, I have disappointed them. Why? Because it was not what I had planned.

We all have plans for our marriages, friendships, relationships, work, our health or our "trophies" as they come in all shapes and sizes. But then, there are those things that upset our expectations and plans. When things do not go the way we planned, perhaps we are shocked or surprised, disappointed or grief stricken or maybe we are just downright angry. We had planned a "perfect" life and something, or someone, jumped in and changed the plans.

Now what do we do with those kinds of disappointments? There are lots of pithy phrases that may get us through a bad day—*"When life hands you lemons, make lemonade"*—but they may not carry you through the anger or disappointment that comes with those unmet expectations.

The book of Proverbs is a fascinating collection of pithy sayings. Thirty-one chapters of insight and wisdom attributed to Solomon. The proverb that starts this meditation instructs the reader to make way for learning by listening. Interestingly, it is coupled with a kind of reflection on "making plans." It says the human heart may make all kinds of plans but, in the end, what really matters is trying to live into God's guidance. Trusting that plans will come out the way we hope often leads to disappointment; trusting in God gives one the ability to be free from the anger of unmet expectations. *"Let go and let God,"* the saying goes. In other words, plans are nice, but God is better than any plan.

The Apostle Paul, as you probably know, did not plan to follow Jesus, but his encounter with the risen Lord changed his plans.[1] He had planned to be one kind of religious leader; he ended up being another kind. He had planned on enjoying the fruits of his success, but wherever he went trouble seemed to meet him, or at the very least be close behind. At life's end, he found himself in prison facing Roman executioners. He had a taste of imprisonment when he was under house arrest in Ephesus. It was here that he wrote one of his most remarkable letters, the very short and power-packed letter to the Philippians. In it, it is clear that Paul has begun to reflect on how his life's plans went asunder. He wrote, *"...I have learned to be content with whatever I have. I know what it is to have little, and I know what it is to have plenty. In any and all circumstances, I have learned the secret of being well-fed and of going hungry, of having plenty and of being in need."* Then he ends by revealing his secret, *"I can do all things through Him who strengthens me."*[2]

1 Acts 9.
2 Philippians 4:11-13.

vas that he knew being linked to God, through His Son ... the power of His Spirit, gave a deep sense of contentment. Not blissful ignorance, or naïve giddiness, but some kind of inward assurance that God would get him through anything and, of course, get us through. When Paul wrote to the Church in Rome, *"We know that all things work together for good for those who love God,"* he did not mean that on the surface "all things worked out good;" he meant that God can "work good in all things."[3] My guess is there are plenty of folks who face the kind of crisis I encountered earlier today. They could tell us right now stories of how God was and is working in their midst, from something as monumental as finding the right physician at the right time to something as miniscule as having a spouse hold their hand when the doctor comes in with the update.

And in your own crisis? God is there. I promise He is there; look around and be patient. Do not let the anger get hold of you and instead hold on to God, because He is surely holding onto you. Hold on to those who come your way, you will see them if you look hard enough. Holding on to both will help you get through those "perfect moments" that did not turn out so perfect. In the end, God will turn it in to its own kind of resurrection, if you just let Him.

And so, let me offer my own pithy phrase from one of my heroines, Corrie Ten Boom, who survived the Ravensbruck concentration camp. My guess is during those dark days, her plans were not coming around quite like she thought. She once said, *"When a train goes through a tunnel and it gets dark, you don't throw away your ticket and jump off. You sit still and trust the engineer."*[4] May I humbly suggest we keep trusting "THE Engineer," even when things do not quite turn out like we planned? In time, He will get you where you need to be.

3 Romans 8:28.
4 This quote was taken from personal notes kept throughout the author's ministry.

Provoking Thought

In what circumstance do you find discontentment right now? When have your plans not turned out as you had hoped? Looking more closely into the circumstance or the changed plan, do you see God's hand? Do you see God's plan? Is His better than yours?

A Prayer for Reflection

Teach me, O God, so to use all the circumstances of my life
Today that they may bring forth in me the fruits of holiness
Rather than the fruits of sin.
Let me use disappointments as material for patience:
Let me use success as material for thankfulness:
Let me use suspense as material for perseverance:
Let me use danger as material for courage:
Let me use reproach as material for longsuffering:
Let me use praise as material for humility:
Let me use pleasure as material for temperance:
Let me use pains as material for endurance.
Amen.

—John Baillie, d. 1960[5]

5 John Baillie, *A Diary of Private Prayer* (New York: Fireside, 1996) 101.

Law and Grace

"For by grace you have been saved through faith, and this is not your own doing; it is the gift of God—not the result of works, so that no one may boast. For we are what he has made us, created in Christ Jesus for good works, which God prepared beforehand to be our way of life."

— Ephesians 2:8-10

After my first year of college, I was scuba diving with three friends off the Gulf Coast of Florida. Due to a series of foolish mistakes, I not only ran out of air at sixty feet below the surface, but when I reached the top with my buddy—who did save my life—we had also become separated from our boat.

Being a young and robust, *foolish* man, I said to my friend, *"Let's just dump the tanks and swim to shore."* Of course I was ignoring the challenges of current, distance, sharks and the reality of my own weakness. My friend chose the better option of staying afloat and yelling for help. A wave carried us high enough for another fishing boat to see the tip of my friend's spear gun waving back and forth in the air. The rest is history.

It was not until I was pulled into the boat that

I realized I really had been rescued, and I played absolutely no role in my rescue except to receive it. It was, and continues to be, a real image of what the Judeo-Christian faith calls grace. When the Apostle Paul writes, *"by grace you have been saved,"* what does that mean? Frankly, it means, there is ***absolutely nothing*** we do that contributes to our salvation.

Earlier on in this little set of meditations, I wrote of the cross where those who flee for forgiveness and redemption receive it—the burned-over place. As we have unpacked other aspects of Christianity in these last several meditations, it is prudent to drop a reminder that much, if not all, of Christianity and its benefits are gifts.

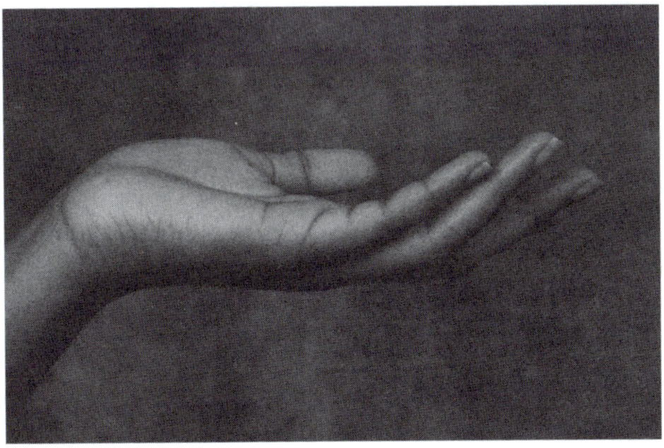

We humans do not like to hear that we get something we have not earned. We tend to have rather inflated views of ourselves and prefer to "win" our way to the trophy, promotion or salary boost. It does not work that way with God's grace. We do not win God's approval by our moral purity, good deeds of Christian charity, theological intellect or religious devotion. Grace says to each of these efforts on our behalf, *"Sorry, It is by grace you are saved, not by **you** that you are saved."*

Certainly our morality, theology, good deeds and religious devotion are part of our life in Christ, but such actions grow out of our love for Christ, not as an attempt to win Him over. In much the same way, certain expressions of marriage (mutual support, intimacy, the building of a family) or friendship (communication, companionship) are not what make the marriage or friendship. It is the love that serves as the greatest cord that binds, and the rest are cords that grow out from this one. If my friendships or marriage depended on my fulfilling my "duties," I would fail miserably and live under the constant burden of *"Am I doing it right?"*

It is a good thing that my salvation does not depend on me. If I were to pile up the good and bad alongside one another, I think the scales would tip more toward the manure in the garden than the flowers I have grown. That is just the way it is. The answer? I have to turn the whole garden over to "The Gardener." That is why the only part we play is to receive. Paul writes, *"by grace... through faith."* The grace is God's work, the faith is how we receive His work. To suggest otherwise is an insult to the death of Christ and I do not think that is too hard of a word.

In his book, *The Grace of God,* William MacDonald puts it this way:

> *To seek to earn, merit, or purchase salvation is to insult the Giver. Imagine yourself invited to a banquet in the White House by the President of The United States. You are seated at a table that is filled with the choicest foods. Every effort is made to give you a most enjoyable evening. At the end of a lovely visit, the President stands at the front door to bid you good-bye.*
>
> *What do you do? As you leave, do you press a dime into his hand and say "Thank you very much for your kindness. I have enjoyed the evening very much. I realize it has cost you a lot of money, and I want to help you pay for the meal."*
>
> *Is that the proper response to his kindness? On the contrary it is a rude and insulting gesture. So it would be with God's grace.*[1]

The real difference here is between law and grace. Winning our way to God's favor via the law means I will never get there. If I had depended on myself alone to get me out of that mess in the Gulf, I would be as dead as the dodo bird. Grace says we already have God's favor, and when we receive that via faith, we are rescued and new life begins, as it was when I was rescued both by my diving buddy and the captain of our little boat. That is the Gospel, plain and simple.

Kenneth Wuest once wrote a little verse that puts it this way:

> *"Do this and live!" the Law demands,*
> *But gives me neither feet nor hands.*
> *A better word God's grace does bring,*
> *It bids me fly and gives me wings.*[2]

And thank God for that. I think I will take grace over law any day. How about you?

---

1 William MacDonald, *The Grace of God* (Kansas City: ECS Ministries, 1960) pamphlet.

2 Kenneth Wuest, *Romans in the Greek New Testament.* Vol. 2 (Eerdmans, 1955) 378.

Provoking Thought

Think on some ways you might try and "earn" God's love. How does it change your view of things to know that God loves you already?

A Prayer for Reflection

Amazing grace! How sweet the sound,
That saved a wretch like me!
I once was lost but now am found,
Was blind but now I see.

'Twas grace that taught my heart to fear,
and grace my fears relieved;
how precious did that grace appear
the hour I first believed.[3]

—John Newton, d. 1807

3 From the hymn, *Amazing Grace*, stanzas 1 and 2.

Be Holy

"Beloved, while eagerly preparing to write to you about the salvation we share, I find it necessary to write and appeal to you to contend for the faith that was once for all entrusted to the saints. For certain intruders have stolen in among you, people who long ago were designated for this condemnation as ungodly, who pervert the grace of our God into licentiousness and deny our only Master and Lord, Jesus Christ."

—Jude 1:3-4

At summer camp once, I accidentally stepped dead onto a wooden splinter that went right into the ball of my foot. To this day, I can still hear my own 12-year-old voice interrupted only by my hopping about, yelling *"Take it out! Take it out!"* The first aid I received was from a 16-year-old counselor who pulled the small spear out with a pair of pliers, told me that I should wash the foot and get back to play time.

About ten days later, I stepped on that spot in just the right way that sent a sharp pain all the way up into my leg. I pulled off my shoes and socks, took a look and it was badly infected! This time I went to the camp nurse who promptly gave me a tongue depressor, told me to turn my head and hold on, because she was out of Novocain and would have to dig out what was evidently the remaining part of the javelin! She was successful and I have the scar to prove it.

Until I got all of the problem out, I was going to have to keep dealing with that initial infection. Infection and a healthy body just simply do not go hand in hand.

The book of Jude is only one chapter and actually, it's a letter. We are not sure who wrote it. Some have thought perhaps Jesus' brother; others think it might be the "other Judas."[1] In any case, it was an early Church leader who was fighting a growing problem in the early days of Christianity. The belief was that somehow, because one had encountered the grace of Christ, they were already "saved," so why not behave as they wanted! If one is already "in" with God, then really, does it matter what one does with his or her body, or mind? Well, evidently yes.

This thinking was an outgrowth of the popular Gnostic movement. The budding religion embraced several Christian doctrines, but also held that the body (the literal, fleshy body) was so corrupt and evil that it could never possibly be good or holy. But suffice it to say, that since Gnosticism shared some of the tenets of Christianity, it was possible for Gnostics to slip into the Christian community. A religion that teaches that you can have your head in the clouds and your feet in the brothel was very attractive to others.

That kind of thinking does not square with Christ. So Jude answers the challenge clearly, *"intruders... pervert the grace of God*

1 Luke 6:16; Acts 1:13.

into licentiousness." In short, no, grace does not mean "free pass." As noted in the last meditation, grace is a gift all around, but it is a gift that should prompt a change in us, in our behavior, thinking, lifestyle, ethics, morals and so on.

An outgrowth of a relationship with God in Christ is a holy life. Peter, evidently battling Gnosticism as well, reached into the Old Testament to remind Christians scattered throughout the ancient civilized world that God was clear about this holiness business, *"Instead, as He who called you is holy, be holy yourselves in all your conduct; for it is written, 'You shall be holy, for I am holy.'"*[2]

Some days ago, we touched upon some issues related to forgiveness. There is no question God forgives, and forgives aplenty. In the last meditation, I touched on some thinking around grace. But forgiveness, and the grace from which it springs, is not a green light to live as one pleases. Christians are called to more than that.

You cannot continue to live with part of the infection left in the body. If you do, in time the infection just grows and eventually consumes. That is really part of that invitation of grace. It says, *"Here it is... it is given not because you scored points with Me [God], but because I love you and do not want you to live in the vicious cycle of sin and guilt. So I forgive you, and as I do, out of my love, I hope your love for Me will grow and effect a change so that what you want more and more is not the infection, but the antibiotic."*

Jude and Peter were right to try and convince early Christians that loving God meant doing more than going to church and Bible Study; it meant, and means, a changed life. Not a perfect one, grace and forgiveness abound, but a holy one. A life that seeks to be healed more than destroyed, filled more than emptied, strengthened more than weakened and made whole more than being infected.

2 I Peter 1:16; Leviticus 11:45.

Provoking Thought

Where have you left some of the splinter in? Perhaps it is time to pull the rest out and hand it over to the grace of God.

A Prayer for Reflection

Almighty God, unto whom all hearts are open, all desires known, and from whom no secrets are hid: Cleanse the thoughts of our hearts by the inspiration of thy Holy Spirit, that we may perfectly love thee, and worthily magnify thy holy Name; through Christ our Lord.[3]

— From *The Book of Common Prayer*

3 *The Book of Common Prayer* 323.

Bearing Fruit

"You did not choose me but I chose you. And I appointed you to go and bear fruit, fruit that will last..."

—John 15:16

I am not a big fan of going to the mall. Aside from the crowds, and the general hullabaloo, I sometimes wince at the interaction between parents and children, wives and husbands, boyfriends and girlfriends. The wince comes when I hear a string of harsh words. I am not writing about the occasional discipline that may be necessary, and perhaps my reader joins me in confessing that I have lost my temper in a long shopping line at one time or another. No, I am talking about something much more severe.

For instance, not too long ago I was walking in front of a mother who was inappropriately and harshly speaking to her young son, perhaps no more than seven years old, putting him down not once, but several times. As I left the mall later, I heard one more parent severely scolding his child. I looked at a young lady in one of the mall kiosks and said, *"I bet you see some very difficult things."* She answered, *"All the time."*

You know, as I have pointed out in these last few meditations, we are not called to be perfect, but we are called to live the law of love with our fellow humans. The Scriptures tell us the fuel that allows this to happen is the Holy Spirit of God, given to us at that point when we come into relationship with our Lord Christ.

Now any of you reading also know that living the law of love can be a daily challenge—often difficult for all kinds of reasons. But we are told that if we walk with our Lord, in time, it will begin to show up in all kinds of ways.

Perhaps that is why the Apostle Paul uses the imagery of a fruit to describe some of the "produce" of a Spirit-filled life, *"...the fruit of the Spirit is love, joy, peace, patience, kindness, goodness, faithfulness, gentleness and self-control."*[1] That is a pretty good list, like a kind of maintenance check for the condition of our souls. Unlike "spiritual gifts" (next meditation) which seem to be parceled out differently to different people, these "fruits" are to be exhibited in the Christian life day to day.

How does one do that? Well, look at your life. Do you see "fruits" growing, popping out, not as a Herculean effort on your part, but *naturally?* If not, then go to your knees in a time of silence and begin to work out and wrestle with those areas of your life not yet submitted to Christ. Sometimes the end result is a big change, a full blown lifestyle conversion. Sometimes it is simply a decision to begin living in one way over another.

I had a colleague in ministry who told me that once he had reached a point of frustration in living out the fruits of goodness in his own life. A particular set of circumstances seemed to say to him that living in a loving way with others really made no difference. Early in his ministry, this frustration hit a peak on one particular day and he angrily stormed into the office of his priest. He said, and I quote, *"I have spent 32 years being a nice person and where has it gotten me!?"* At which point, his priest said, *"Would you like to spend the rest of your life as an angry person?" "No,"* my friend answered. *"Then choose nice!"* his priest said. I am happy to tell you he did.

I am not perfect and cannot promise anyone with whom I share life that there will not be days when I am rather fruitless. But I know accepting the grace of Christ into our lives and the Spirit that comes with that, does give us the power to, in Jesus' words, *"bear fruit."* If we let them live in and through us, I bet the mall would be a better place to visit.

Why not take the counsel of that wise old priest? Let us choose the fruits of the Spirit. Well?

---

1 Galatians 5:22-23.

Provoking Thought

Take a look at the list of Paul's fruits. Where do you fall short? Which ones do you see popping out? So what will you choose?

A Prayer for Reflection

O God, thou has commanded us to walk in the Spirit and not to fulfill the lusts of the flesh; make us perfect, we pray, in love, that we may conquer our natural selfishness and give ourselves to others. Fill our hearts with thy joy, and garrison them with thy peace; make us long-suffering and gentle, and thus subdue our hasty and angry tempers; give us faithfulness, meekness and self-control; that so crucifying the flesh with its affections and lusts, we may bring forth the fruit of the Spirit to thy praise and glory; through Jesus Christ our Lord. Amen.

— Henry Alford, d. 1871
Former Dean of Canterbury Cathedral[2]

2 Counsell 362-363.

Living Sacrifices

"I appeal to you therefore, brothers and sisters, by the mercies of God, to present your bodies as a living sacrifice, holy and acceptable to God, which is your spiritual worship... For as in one body we have many members, and not all the members have the same function, so we, who are many, are one body in Christ, and individually we are members one of another. We have gifts that differ according to the grace given to us: prophecy, in proportion to faith; ministry, in ministering; the teacher, in teaching; the exhorter, in exhortation; the giver, in generosity; the leader, in diligence; the compassionate, in cheerfulness."

— Romans 12:1, 4-8

In my wife's family, we really have an "Aunt Bea." I have been the beneficiary, like hundreds of others, of her hospitality. By hospitality, I do not mean simply staying over for a good meal and a warm bed. I mean an open and generous house to which you are welcomed, made to feel special, nothing is expected but your pleasure and joy in visiting, eating and taking delight in being tended to by one who has an extraordinary gift of hospitality.

My wife and I enjoy having people over, and when all the plans are carefully made, we love opening our home. That is what one might call "regular hospitality." What flows out of the heart of Aunt Bea is an extraordinary, some might say supernatural, gift of hospitality. You can show up at Aunt Bea's almost any hour of any day and you would be welcomed with open arms. The same is not true of my home—you might be welcomed—or I might switch off the porch light depending on the time of the night.

In the New Testament, we find several places where "gifts" of the Holy Spirit are described.[1] Now gifts, unlike fruits (as I described in the last meditation) are unique to the person. Spiritual fruits are a natural outgrowth of a relationship with Christ; gifts are given to people as God so chooses. In other words, one may have hospitality (like Aunt Bea); one may have teaching. The extraordinary, particular gift exercised through Christians is called the "Gift of the Spirit." It is, in a very real sense, a kind of miracle—a glimpse into the Kingdom and power of God.

There are three important pieces one should take hold of around these gifts. First, it is a gift. So you can take pride in it if you choose, but if it was handed to you by the One who designed the gift, picked you to receive it, and counts on you to use it—would it not be better just to thank the Giver, point to the Giver, and use the gift in a way that glorifies the Giver?

Second, it is important to identify your gift(s). For this, you may need to seek the counsel of your priest or pastor. You may need to pray and reflect on those things which seem to come natural to you, but not so natural to others. You may also need to be honest about gifts you *do not have*. If you do not have the gift of teaching, then why try? Better to use the gift you have been given than to try and pretend like you have one you do not.

Thirdly, use your gift. Paul implores the Christians in ancient Rome to present themselves as "living sacrifices." That means they should pour out their lives, using the gifts they have been given, to others and to God. If we fast-forward to today, Paul's plea tells us when it comes to our own spiritual gifts we should not hoard, hide, reject, resent or ignore our gift, but use it. Use it to God's glory and for the benefit

1 I Corinthians 12; Isaiah 11:1-5; Ezekiel 11:19; Psalm 127:3; I Corinthians 7:7; Philippians 4:7; Hebrews 4:1, 9; James 1:5, 4:6.

of God's people, and perhaps even for those who do not seem to have much use for God. Perhaps, through you and your gifts, they would be drawn to Him.

The pastor and devotional writer, Chuck Swindoll, likes to tell of an encounter he had with one man's spiritual gift. He writes, *"My life has been crossed by men who have the gift of giving. Maybe yours has also. When I was at Dallas Seminary, God used a man in my life and in the lives of ten other fellows at the school. [He] chose to underwrite our tuition. Absolutely unsolicited. Each time tuition came due, there was a check in the mail.*

"I remember one time he came to Dallas and got all eleven of us together and said, 'I want us to take a drive downtown.' After a sandwich, he took us several blocks away to a men's store. Inside he suited us up in new suits, new sports coats, one fellow after another. He sat there and just beamed! He was happier than we were! He wasn't wealthy, but there was something inside of him (it's called a spiritual gift) that was not satisfied until there was an outlet for that gift."[2]

So once you have found it, what to do? Respond, with all you are, to Paul's invitation, *"I appeal to you therefore, brothers and sisters, by the mercies of God, to present your bodies as a living sacrifice."*

2 Charles R. Swindoll, *The Tale Of The Tardy Oxcart* (Nashville: Thomas Nelson, 1998) 533.

Provoking Thought

Review the list of spiritual gifts and see if you can discern your gift or gifts. If so, are you putting them to work? If not, why not?

A Prayer for Reflection

Almighty and eternal God, so draw our hearts to thee, so guide our minds, so fill our imaginations, so control our wills, that we may be wholly Thine, utterly dedicated unto thee; and then use us, we pray thee, as thou wilt, but always to thy glory and the welfare of thy people, through our Lord and Savior, Jesus Christ.

— William Temple, d. 1944
Archbishop of Canterbury[3]

3 Batchelor 95.

Godsequence

"But they and our ancestors acted presumptuously and stiffened their necks and did not obey your commandments; they refused to obey, and were not mindful of the wonders that you performed among them; but they stiffened their necks and determined to return to their slavery in Egypt. But you are a God ready to forgive, gracious and merciful, Slow to anger and abounding in steadfast love, and you did not forsake them."

— Nehemiah 9:16-17

One of the great benefits of my vocation is to be able to witness miracles. I remember the call I got when I learned one of my mentors had been diagnosed with a terminal illness, and yet, after a period of treatment and more prayers than anyone could number, he went into full remission.

Another time, one of my parishioners who was a politician early in life and by his own confession had made many enemies, was diagnosed with liver cancer and given only months to live. However, to the amazement of his doctors and family members, he actually lived over two years. This gave him the opportunity to make peace with everyone he had hurt during a darker season of his life.

Such miracles that happen in the lives of others, but not in our own, may prompt us to think "What about my friend? Or spouse, child, parent or me?" who also has cancer and seems to be getting worse. Does God love them more than He loves me? No. Let me script it again—***no.***

Over my years of pastoral ministry, I have prayed with folks who had chronic or terminal illnesses, people who were, for a time, delivered from the disease and even certain death. I have also prayed with other people who seemingly got worse than when we began, and eventually died. Why? Why do some seem to squeak by and some do not? Why do some get to cross the goal line and spike the ball and others leave the field altogether?

Let me offer a few caveats first before we tackle that question. First, it is probably important to keep in mind that no one gets out of this world and to the next alive. Every person Jesus raised from the dead, even Lazarus, had to die again.

Second, I do very much believe in miracles and I believe in the power of prayer to affect such miracles. But miracles do not always occur in the way *I* would like them to occur, and prayers are not always answered the way *I* would like them to be. For instance, I have had people with terminal illness tell me that they would receive their death as a blessed release and indeed, actually a miracle.

So back to that question—why do miracles seem selective? Holy Scripture suggests to us that miracles have one purpose, to point us back to God. Now there are miracles every single day, despite our best efforts to work against it. As John Claypool used to tell me, *"God is always changing water to wine, just a bit slower than at the wedding in Cana of Galilee!"* But, then there are the big ones—someone is healed, another escapes disaster, a business unexpectedly turns around—the list goes on.

Scholars cannot seem to agree on who actually wrote the Old Testament book of Nehemiah, but they are fairly certain it was the same person who wrote I and II Chronicles and a sequel entitled Ezra. The point of the little series is to accurately chronicle a period of ancient Israel's history. In the passage above, the author is writing to God about a time when the Jews, through a series of miracles, had been freed from Pharaoh's Egyptian captivity. But no sooner had they

been freed, they forgot the wonderful miracles God had done!

Miracles are not about you or me, who gets one and who does not. Miracles are about God. C.S. Lewis wrote, *"Miracles in fact are retelling in small letters of the very same story which is written across the whole world in letters too large for some of us to see."*[1] The miracles remind us that there is Someone much bigger, much more important than us. And they point us, again and again, to the One who created us, redeems us and sustains us.

If a miracle occurs, and we brush it off as just a coincidence, then we have missed its point. As Archbishop William Temple once said, *"All I know is the more I pray, the more coincidences there are in my life."*

The more we pray, the more we have the eyes to see, the more miracles we will also see. Some of them arrive with supernatural fanfare like healing, restoration of a broken marriage or friendship, an insight that saves the business. Some of them arrive rather quietly like the small voice of friendship, the joy of a lover's kiss, the silence of the setting sun and at times, even death.

So I am very grateful to be able to witness all kinds of miracles, which I believe not to be a consequence—but perhaps a Godsequence—a reminder that recipients of such gifts are not the only ones who are special to God, but we all are.

1 C. S. Lewis, *God in the Dock*. Ed. Walter Hooper (Grand Rapids: Eerdmans, 1972) 29.

Provoking Thought

When is the last time you witnessed a miracle? Maybe you are witnessing one now; watch for it.

A Prayer for Reflection

I asked for strength that I might achieve;
I was made weak that I might learn humbly to obey.
I asked for health that I might do greater things;
I was given infirmity that I might do better things.
I asked for riches that I might be happy;
I was given poverty that I might be wise.
I asked for power that I might have the praise of men;
I was given weakness that I might feel the need of God.
I asked for all things that I might enjoy life;
I was given life that I might enjoy all things.
I got nothing that I had asked for,
But everything that I had hoped for.
Almost despite myself, my unspoken prayers were answered;
I am, among all men, most richly blessed.

— Unknown Confederate soldier, 1865[2]

2 Counsell 429-430.

Unforbidden Fruit

"Beloved, let us love one another, because love is from God; everyone who loves is born of God and knows God. Whoever does not love does not know God, for God is love. God's love was revealed among us in this way: God sent His only Son into the world so that we might live through Him. In this is love, not that we loved God but that He loved us and sent His Son to be the atoning sacrifice for our sins. Beloved, since God loved us so much, we also ought to love one another. No one has ever seen God; if we love one another, God lives in us, and his love is perfected in us."

— I John 4:7-12

The Holy Spirit. The Fruits of the Spirit. The Gifts of the Spirit. How about "unforbidden fruit?"

I suppose we preachers are accused of spending more time than necessary pointing out the "forbidden fruits." For just a moment, I want you to ponder a very important, unforbidden fruit. What is it?

As we saw a few meditations back, Paul lists several fruits of the Holy Spirit that are planted in the heart of the Christian believer. Through God's grace and our personal devotion, these fruits take root and grow. Tucked into Paul's list is clearly an unforbidden fruit... love.

Recently, in my own study, I read back through what is known as John's Epistles (I, II and III John). These are beautiful letters, written by the same author of John's Gospel, as well as the book of Revelation. As John begins to pen these letters, the church and its body of Christians

is beginning to feel the full brunt of persecution. John is clear throughout his letters that it is important to be grounded in the faith, and to constantly weed out evil as it perks up its head both in one's individual life, or the Church itself. But how interesting too, that soaked throughout these three letters is the constant reference to live in love, express love and be children of love.

Facing a world that literally was hating the followers of Jesus, John does not suggest a return of evil for evil, to take up arms or even to turn away but to continue to love. Here is another important piece of Scripture, *"For this is the message you heard from the beginning, that we should love one another... Do not be surprised, brothers and sisters, that the world hates you... This is how we know love: Jesus Christ laid down his life for us—and we ought to lay down our lives for our brothers and sisters... Dear children, let us not love with words or tongue but with actions and in truth."*[1]

Now there are day-to-day reasons we do not act in a loving way—we are tired or stressed, money is tight, the boss is on our back, we have a headache! I suppose most of us have had those moments. But when we fail to act in a loving way as a general characteristic, then something is amiss.

So a deeper reason that we may fail to enjoy this unforbidden fruit is that we have forgotten how much we are loved. Love, unconditional and generous love, is a remedy to virtually all our emotional and spiritual ills. When someone refuses to love, it is often because they have not experienced it themselves. Many people come from faulty and broken homes where real love was something bruised and bent at best. These people lose a sense of self-worth and security that would naturally come with an innate sense that regardless of anything, there is Someone there who cares about you.

1 I John 3:11, 13, 16, 18.

Perhaps that is why John also writes, *"See what love the Father has given us, that we should be called children of God; and that is what we are!"*[2] Oh, if we could let that good word sink down into our souls, then regardless of childhood, work environment or general disposition, we could begin to feast on, as well as share with others, the unforbidden fruit of love.

Not altogether sure what it looks like? There is a chapter in Paul's First Letter to the Church in Corinth that is often called "The Love Chapter." You have probably heard parts of it read at weddings. I think in it, as a description of love, Paul hits the nail on the head, *"Love is patient; love is kind; love is not envious or boastful or arrogant or rude. It does not insist on its own way; it is not irritable or resentful; it does not rejoice in wrongdoing but rejoices in the truth. It bears all things, believes all things, hopes all things, endures all things. Love never ends."*[3] Pause for a moment, review the list. Is this how you express love to your friends, spouse, children, coworkers, fellow Church members?

Now none of us can perfectly love; only One did this. But it should be growing in us, and if it is not, then we need to go back to the Source, Jesus Christ. Have you opened your heart fully to His love? Have you invited Him to come and take up residence? Is He Lord and Savior, and not just somebody in Sunday school stories? If you can answer "yes" to these questions, then love is planted and it will grow. But if the answer is "no" or "I'm not really sure," then perhaps it is time to allow Christ past the perimeter of your life, into the very core.

Need some of that fruit? Take a big bite. Because once you do, it will begin to nourish you and, in turn, you will be able to turn over your own fruit basket into those hungry souls around you and feed them with that fruit that, thanks be to God, is unforbidden.

2 I John 3:1.
3 I Corinthians 13:4-8a.

Provoking Thought

Have you, do you, experience the love of God? Do you know how much God loves you? How can you more fully share that love with others? If you are reticent to do so, what is it that stops you?

A Prayer for Reflection

O God, I seek a love that is already there; I want to know a love that is already present; help me in my frailty and self-centeredness to open my heart to your love. Fill me afresh so that made whole with that love, I may share it with all You send my way. In the name of God, Whose other name is Love. Amen.

— RJL+

Tilling the Soil

"Hear, O Israel: The Lord is our God, the Lord alone. You shall love the Lord your God with all your heart, and with all your soul, and with all your might. Keep these words that I am commanding you today in your heart."

— Deuteronomy 6:4-6

The passage above is known by Jews as the great *Shema*—a kind of singular law of the land that Moses tried to impress into the minds of the Jews who were making their way from a life of bondage in Egypt to a life of freedom in the Promised Land. Jesus pulled from the *Shema* one day when He was asked which was the greatest of all laws. He responded, *"'You shall love the Lord your God with all your heart, and with all your soul, and with all your mind.' This is the greatest and first commandment. And a second one is like it, 'You shall love your neighbor as yourself.' On these two commandments hang all the law and the prophets."*[1]

Now, as suggested in the last meditation, inviting that love into one's heart is a good starting place for living out the law of love—that "unforbidden fruit." But as was also suggested, that fruit has a tendency to grow when nurtured by a disciplined life of spiritual devotion. There are lots of ways this can happen, but over the next few meditations, I want to focus simply on four: study and humility before the Holy Scriptures, prayer, worship and service. These are not listed in any particular order. All of them require personal sacrifice, a willingness to give up something and take something on. In a practical way, we must give up time to spend time doing something that not many people in today's world would fully appreciate, but

1 Matthew 22:36-40; Mark 12:28-31.

also in a submissive way, we must come seeking to receive what these acts of devotion may have for us.

When I was in seminary, I had some professors who constantly felt it was their duty to push back against the conventional, perhaps traditional, teachings of our Judeo-Christian faith. They were constantly looking for the new spin on our beliefs, and in some instances, suggested tossing aside those things that no longer seemed to serve a purpose in the modern world. But a submissive willingness to be moved, changed, taught, helped, comforted, afflicted and finally transformed by the experiences of giving oneself to personal devotion is an important pathway to living in a way that honors God.

Before the Middle Ages, the only way farmers had to till the soil was with mules and thin, light rakes that just skimmed across the ground. This process, called "skittering," merely turned over the topsoil, such that when seeds were scattered, it was hard for them to set in, and grow down. For obvious reasons, skittering yielded a fairly anemic harvest.

When iron became a more frequent piece of the agricultural landscape, large, heavy and thick blades could be hauled behind not just one, but a team of oxen. The blades would go down deep and really turn over the soil. It was taxing work as farmers would encounter rabbit holes, wasps' nests and, more frustratingly, rocks and roots for which they had to stop and start over. This came to be known as deep plowing. It required longer hours, and harder work, but then the seeds went down deeper where the soil was richer and, of course, the harvest was much more bountiful than during those old days of skittering.

Grace, as already suggested, is a gift of God. Like any gift, it is something that requires tending and care, almost constant attention. If we are willing to allow that love to go much deeper into us, it may be taxing and even painful at times. It may turn up old roots, stones and wasps' nests, but once they are out of the way, the avenue is clear for the love of God to go much deeper. Of course, when that happens, the harvest is always plentiful!

Provoking Thought

As we prepare to look at just a few avenues of spiritual devotion, where do you feel the "brakes coming on"? Where do you feel resistance? Why? Why do you think that is the case?

A Prayer for Reflection

Now it is You alone that I love,
You alone that I follow,
You alone that I seek,
You alone that I feel ready to serve,
Because You alone rule justly,
It is to Your authority alone that I want to submit,
Command me, I pray, to do whatever You will,
But heal and open my ears
That I may hear Your voice.
Heal and open my eyes
That I may see your will,
Drive out from me
All fickleness,
That I may acknowledge you alone.
Tell me where to look
That I may see you,
And I will place my hope in doing your will.
Amen.

— St. Augustine, d. 430[2]

2 Batchelor 395.

To Pray

"He was praying in a certain place, and after he had finished, one of his disciples said to him, 'Lord, teach us to pray, as John taught his disciples.' He said to them, 'When you pray, say:
Father, hallowed be your name.
Your kingdom come.
Give us each day our daily bread.
And forgive us our sins,
for we ourselves forgive everyone indebted to us.
And do not bring us to the time of trial."

— Luke 11:1-4

One way in which we begin to more deeply break the topsoil of our lives so that God can do a bit of deep planting within us is prayer. Prayer, that crucial link of communication between human and the Divine, is one of the primary ways that God speaks to us and we can speak to Him. In my vocation, I have found that people pray in all kinds of ways, places and with all kinds of words and actions. I have included in these meditations a kind of hodge-podge of prayers from a variety of Christians. A quick skim would show you the kind of variety that I mean. I do not think the how, where and why is nearly as important as the simple *do.*

My wife and I recently toured a traveling *Titanic* exhibit. It tells once again that infamous and ominous story through a collection of photos and many actual artifacts that were scooped up from the ocean's floor in the north Atlantic. Plates looking as if they just came out of a dishwasher, clothes, a chandelier, tuxedo buttons and a child's toy plane. Also included was a piece of sheet music, stained with salt water, but the title and most of the words could still be read.

On the sheet was a song that many believed was included in the collection of pieces played by the now well-known string quartet that performed even as the ship began its descent. The words at the heading, *"Teach Us to Pray."* My guess is that there were many that were praying on that desperate night. Perhaps some who were quite familiar with the language of prayer, some who prayed every now and then, some who were thinking, *"Teach us to pray."* Here is the text attributed to James Montgomery:

Lord, teach us how to pray aright

Lord, teach us how to pray aright,
with reverence and with fear;
though dust and ashes in thy sight,
we may, we must draw near.

We perish if we cease from prayer,
O grant us power to pray!
And when to meet thee we prepare,
Lord, meet us by the way.

God of all grace, we bring to thee
a broken, contrite heart;
give, what thine eye delights to see,
truth in the inward part.

Faith in the only sacrifice
that can for sin atone;
to build our hopes, to fix our eyes,
on Christ, on Christ alone;

Patience to watch and wait and weep,
though mercy long delay;
courage our fainting souls to keep,
and trust thee though thou slay.

Give these, and then thy will be done;
thus strengthened with all might,
we through thy Spirit and thy Son,
shall pray, and pray aright.[1]

Interesting to me, in the little scene from above, Jesus responds to an inquiry about prayer with the words, *"When you pray."* Not *"If you pray"* or *"When you get around to prayer,"* but *"When you pray."* It was understood, an expectation and part of the business of being a disciple.

Philip Yancey, in writing on prayer, notes, *"The psychiatrist Gerald C. May observed, 'After twenty years of listening to the yearnings of people's hearts, I am convinced that human beings have an inborn desire for God.*

Whether we are consciously religious or not, this desire is our deepest longing and most precious treasure.' Surely, if we are made in God's own image, God will find a way to fulfill that deepest longing. Prayer is that way."[2]

I would suggest you not wait until an emergency, but that you continue to foster the language of prayer as one of those open doors to a deeper relationship with our Lord. The Apostles were not alone in their desire to know how to pray. Maybe we are more like them than we would be willing to admit or even realize.

So, not if, but *when* you pray, you might need a little help along the way. On your knees is a good place to start, then perhaps just begin as the Apostles did, *"Lord... teach us to pray."* Indeed, *"we perish if we cease from prayer, O grant us power to pray!"*

1 Poem by James Montgomery, 1819.
2 Philip Yancey, *Prayer: Does It Make Any Difference?* (Grand Rapids: Zondervan, 2006) 16.

Provoking Thought

The devotional writer Richard Foster has said that "to pray is to change." What change might prayer bring to your life?

A Prayer for Reflection

Let us not seek out of thee what we can find only in thee, O Lord: peace and rest and joy and bliss, which abide in thee alone.

Lift up our souls above the weary round of harassing thoughts to Thy eternal presence.

Lift up our minds to the pure, bright, serene, light of Thy presence, that there we may repose in Thy love and be at rest from ourselves and all things that weary us; and thence return, arrayed in Thy peace, to do and to bear whatsoever shall best please thee, O blessed Lord.

— The Reverend Canon E. B. Pusey, d. 1882[3]

3 Batchelor 410.

God-Breathed

"All scripture is inspired by God and is useful for teaching, for reproof, for correction, and for training in righteousness, so that everyone who belongs to God may be proficient, equipped for every good work."

— II Timothy 3:16-17

In the denomination I serve, one of the most moving of all liturgical services is the ordination of a deacon or priest into the service of the church. To me, perhaps one of the most moving pieces of that particular service is when the candidate must pledge, in front of the entire congregation, *"I solemnly declare that I do believe the Holy Scriptures of the Old and New Testaments to be the Word of God and to contain all things necessary to salvation."*[1] After that statement, the candidate must then, in the presence of all gathered, sign a document that attests to the spoken promise.

In addition to prayer, one of the ways God speaks to us is through the Holy Scriptures of the Old and New Testaments. We call them "Holy" because they are, indeed, set apart from all other writings. Every now and then, I encounter someone who says something along the lines of the following to me, *"I don't know why you make such a big deal about the Bible—it's just another book, like any other, written by humans."* To buy into that kind of thinking, or to make that kind of statement, is

1 *The Book of Common Prayer* 538.

tantamount to the examples above. It would require that I turn my back on that crucial promise I made at my own ordination, but also show an arrogant irreverence for the book that has played such a large part in the revelation of our faith and our God.

Humans tend to take great pride in their own knowledge and so, as with prayer, to rest our minds and souls before Scripture requires an element of humility. Many modern folk tend to believe that God treats all modes of revelation equally—poetry, nature, music, literature, theater, even television and film! In part, that is true, because God's revelation can be made known in and through many avenues. But Christians must take a different view of God's revelation through Holy Scripture. Holy Scripture serves as the ethical, moral, theological and spiritual compass for the Christian. Without that compass we are very likely to lose our way and stray far from the path of the Christian journey.

Richard Hooker, a kind of architect of early Protestant faith as it was expressed through Anglicanism, wrote, *"What Scripture doth plainly deliver, to that the first place both of credit and obedience is due; the next whereunto is whatsoever any man can necessarily conclude by force of reason: after these the voice of the Church succeedeth."*[2] In other words, when it comes to receiving Scripture, it speaks plainly first for itself and then can make its way to the lens of human reason and the voice of the church.

There was a moving moment of this view of Holy Scripture that played itself out during the coronation of Queen Elizabeth I. Though arguably the most powerful monarch of her time, she ordered that, as a symbol of her submission to the Bible, the following should take place, *"[A] Bible, translated into English, let down to her on a silken cord by a child representing Truth. Elizabeth, ever mindful of the visually dramatic, kissed both her hands as she reached out to receive it and then kissed the Bible itself and clasped it to her breast. She promised the expectant crowd she would study and learn from it..."*[3]

Thus, we Christians are called to read Holy Scripture as another avenue to knowing God, and allowing Him to move in and dwell in us more securely. If we want to know God, it is important to read His Word. The literal translation of Paul's words from his letter to *Timothy* cited in the opening Scripture, is that *"all Scripture is God-breathed."* Wow.

2 *Ecclesiastical Polity*, 1593-1597.
3 Jane Dunn, *Elizabeth and Mary: Cousins, Rivals, Queens* (New York: Vintage, 2005) 32.

In other words it is a kind of love letter from the Holy One to humankind itself. It tells the story—again and again, in so many ways, of creation, struggle, sin, redemption, and hope for humanity.

The modern Christian will wisely see that some of Scripture is literally true—some is history, some instruction, some letters written from one saint to another, but also acknowledge that some of Scripture is inspired truth spoken through story, metaphor and imagery. We can affirm that some of Scripture applies only to the audience to whom it was addressed or the time in which it was written, and that some of it is just as timely for Christians in this day as it was the day ink was put to parchment.

What the modern Christian cannot do, if he or she wishes to live a Christian life, is to set the Bible on the shelf next to the dictionary and photo albums, to be pulled out only in moments of spiritual desperation.

I have had members of the parishes I have served say to me that they do not read the Bible because they "do not understand it," or "it is too tedious," or "its language is too difficult." No, our excuses for not reading Holy Scripture must be stripped away from the truth like a wrapper from a valuable present. The Bible can and does address our issues of relationships, loneliness, anxiety, emptiness, fear, finances, sexuality, work ethic, taxes and so much more! Theodore Roosevelt once wrote, *"If a man is not familiar with the Bible, he has suffered a loss which he had better make all possible haste to correct."* Good words. Here is another.

Roman monastic Thomas Merton unveiled his own view of Scripture with these powerful words, *"By reading of Scripture, I am so renewed that all nature seems renewed around me and with me. The sky seems to be a purer, cooler blue, the trees a deeper green, light is sharper on the outlines of the forest and the hills and the whole world is charged with the glory of God."* [4]

So where to begin? Call your pastor or priest. Attend a Bible Study. Perhaps most importantly, pick up the Bible and read it daily. Read it slowly, a chapter at a time or maybe just a paragraph at a time. Start simply, perhaps with the Psalms or one of the Gospels. The key is to start.

Pick the Bible up, and open it as if it were a letter from your spouse, your child or, better yet, your great, great, great grandparent! Who would not open and read with eagerness?

St. Ambrose once wrote, *"As in Paradise, God walks in the Holy Scriptures, seeking the human being."* The good news is, if you jump in there and begin to read, the seeking part is over and you get to walk along with the Holy One who is already walking along with you.

Provoking Thought

Pick up and read Psalm 1. What does this one small morsel of Scripture say to you? If you can find some insight into God in this one piece, do you not think there is much more to learn?

A Prayer for Reflection

Blessed Lord, who hast caused all Holy Scriptures to be written for our learning: Grant that we may in such wise hear them, read, mark, learn, and inwardly digest them; that by patience and comfort of thy holy Word, we may embrace and ever hold fast the blessed hope of everlasting life, which thou hast given us in our Savior Jesus Christ; who liveth and reigneth with thee and the Holy Spirit, one God, forever and ever. Amen.

— From *The Book of Common Prayer*[5]

4 These quotes were taken from personal notes kept throughout the author's ministry.
5 *The Book of Common Prayer* 184.

In Holy Splendor

"O Lord, our Sovereign, how majestic is Your name in all the earth! You have set your glory above the heavens."

— Psalm 8:1

A few pages back, we took some time to look at idolatry, particularly as it might reflect a misplaced allegiance in the affections of our heart. One of the ways Christians, and our Jewish forebears, reflected that allegiance was the act of participatory worship. Where to begin?

"Showing up" is really quite important. We are told, in Luke 4:16, that Jesus went to synagogue, *"as was His custom."* My guess is that there were days when the sermon went on a bit too long, someone was hacking away with a cough in the back pew, the reader stumbled on his words, but Jesus still showed up.

Because worship is a reflection of those things in which we place our worth, if our Lord and showing Him respect is important to you, then you would certainly show up. What if you knew the Queen of England would be in church next Sunday? How many of you might scramble to get a seat? What if your favorite film star, sports figure or author were speaking? Would you make an extra effort to be there?

Well, there is Someone who shows up every week. He is much more important than a political or public figure—He is God, the Creator of the universe, the Redeemer of humankind. Of course, at any place you may choose to worship, there are days when it may seem like God may not be there—the sermon may be boring, the sound just a bit off, the hymn may be unfamiliar. But you know, it really is not about the "how"; it is about the "who." And if Jesus is important to you, then spending time in worship of Him will be as well.

Keeping in mind then that worship is about that "who" and not "how," I sometimes learn much on the receiving end of my work. Every now and then, someone comes up to me and says, *"I don't like that hymn,"* or *"I really don't like that communion prayer"* or *"Why don't we use a different version of the Bible that I prefer?"* Notice what all those statements have in common? ***"I."*** Now, it is true that in our worship we should certainly be attentive to things that turn the worshipper off from drawing closer to our Lord, and things that may also help one worship. Primarily, worship is about Christ, not about the congregation.

As James Torrance puts it, *"When we focus on the question of who, we can rejoice together as we look away from ourselves to Him, that He may sanctify us and lead us together into the presence of the Holy Father."*[1] Thus, an important element in worship is making sure we do not think so much about what "I" may want; instead, focus on Jesus and then I think you will see very much how the words, hymns, music and liturgy will be a reflection of your love for Him.

I know some reader may be asking, *"Can't **I** just do all of this at home?"* I recently read of a little Victorian scene when a clergyman went to call on one of his members who had stopped going to church. They were sitting in front of a roaring fire when the parishioner said, *"Why can't **I** just stay at home and worship God in my own way?!"* Without saying a word, the priest went over to the fire, opened the screen and

1 James B. Torrance, *Worship, Community & the Triune God of Grace* (New York: InterVarsity, 1997) 92.

began to separate the piled up coals that were providing the light and warmth of the fire. He moved each one out from another until they were set alone along the grate. As he did, the fire began to die down, and the warmth in the room nearly went away. His member got the point and decided to start showing up again the next week.

Like prayer and like reading of Holy Scripture, worship is a matter of acting on our desire to be an authentic disciple of Jesus Christ. It gives us an opportunity to brush up to God's presence. David, the author of so many of our wonderful hymns, poems and songs of praise, reminds God's people that this brushing up against God is one of those heart-shifting experiences that grow out of worship, *"Ascribe to the Lord the glory due His name; bring an offering and come before Him. Worship the Lord in holy splendor; tremble before Him, all the earth."*[2]

When all is said and done, worship gives us the opportunity to allow that fire of Christ to burn just a bit brighter within us and around us. Just go sit, kneel, listen, pray, recite. Let it be your custom, as it was for Jesus. When you do gather, remember that it is about Him.

2 I Chronicles 16:29-30.

Provoking Thought

What, if anything, keeps you from being a regular participant in worship? What is the real reason? If you do worship on a regular basis, how can you more fully invest yourself in the experience?

A Prayer for Reflection

Almighty God, we will come into Thy house, even upon the multitude of thy mercies, and in Thy fear will we worship toward Thy holy Temple. Hear the voice of our humble petitions, when we cry unto Thee, when we hold up our hands towards Thy mercy-seat. Let Thine eyes be open, and let Thine ears be attentive to hearken unto the prayer which Thy servants pray toward the place, whereof Thou hast said, that Thou wouldest put thy name there; for the sake of Jesus Christ. Amen.

— Lancelot Andrewes, d. 1626
Bishop of Chichester, Ely and Winchester[3]

3 Counsell 229.

Let the Service Begin

"When the Son of Man comes in His glory, and all the angels with Him, then He will sit on the throne of His glory. All the nations will be gathered before Him, and He will separate people one from another as a shepherd separates the sheep from the goats, and He will put the sheep on his right hand and the goats at the left. Then the king will say to those at his right hand, 'Come you that are blessed by my Father, inherit the kingdom prepared for you from the foundation of the world; for I was hungry and you gave me food, I was thirsty and you gave me something to drink, I was a stranger and you welcomed me, I was naked and you gave me clothing, I was sick and you visited me... Truly I tell you, just as you did it to one of the least of these who are members of my family, you did it to me.'"

— Matthew 25:31-36, 40

For five years of my ordained ministry, I served a wonderful parish in Lafayette, Louisiana. It was my first season as a rector, so years of study and apprenticeship were now going to have to come forward to present themselves as practical and applicable.

Having spent my entire life up to that point east of the Mississippi, I was (primarily due to my own lack of preparation) thrust into what many know to be a unique culture. It is one thing to eat and enjoy Cajun cuisine or listen and dance to zydeco music. It is quite another to move into the region that birthed them. I did not know what *boudin* or *cracklin'* was. I had never seen a nutria outside my office window or an armadillo in my front yard. I had never lived in a city where names like Melancon and Boudreaux were more common than Smith and Jones.

The parish which I was called to lead was very different in its style, size and programs than any of the parishes I had previously assisted. But I was called to serve there and that is what I had to find a way to do—***serve.***

All the prayer, study of Scriptures and worship we do to open ourselves more to the transforming power of the Holy Spirit within us should do more than simply color our beliefs and morals. It should call us to serve others. And service of any kind that is good and holy requires that we get out of ourselves and give of ourselves.

This is what we read unfolding in the Scripture from Matthew. It is one of those broad brush stroke portraits of the end of time that scholars call *apocalyptic literature*. This could be scary stuff, but it is rather clear. Jesus tells His followers that part of following Him means serving the hungry, the thirsty, the stranger, the naked, those in prison and so on. Serve others in this condition and you are serving Him.

That first year in Lafayette was a real test of what I had learned in the years of graduate and post-graduate school, and in the relatively safe world of assistantship on a church staff. I could no longer blame others for the direction of the church; I was in that chair that had to ultimately steer the ship one way or another. And what I learned, like any sailor will tell you, is that you cannot steer from the bow; the real direction of the ship is determined by the captain who is willing to steer from the stern where the rudder lives. In other words, I had to be willing to go to the back of the line and serve. I had

to give up some of my preconceived and prejudiced notions about the kinds of things that would work in a parish. I was in a different culture now, and I had to get my own proclivities out of the way and make space for those whom I was to serve.

I did not lose my personality or temperament, nor did I give up my morals or core beliefs. I did not fail to lead when necessary. But more often than not, I had to step back and remember that it was not what "I" wanted that mattered most, but what that one I encountered needed. That should be, at ground zero, the kind of fruit our personal faith should produce. James put it well, *"So faith, by itself, if it has no works, is dead."*[1] Why is that?

Author Gayle Erwin reminds her readers that there are two central seas in Palestine. One is fresh and teeming with life surrounded by lush trees and playing children—life. The River Jordan, she points out, feeds this sea with sparkling water from the nearby hills.

The River Jordan also flows into another sea, where there is no splash of fish and no fluttering leaf, no song birds and no laughter of children. The air over it hangs heavy and neither animal nor human will drink from it.

1 James 2:17.

What makes the mighty difference in these neighboring seas, both of whom are spread by the same river? The River Jordan empties the same good water into both, but here is the difference: The Sea of Galilee receives, but does not keep the Jordan. For every drop that flows into it, another drop flows out. What goes into the sea goes out in equal measure.

"The other sea is shrewder, hoarding its income jealously. It will not be tempted into any generous impulse. Every drop it gets it keeps," she writes. *"The Sea of Galilee gives and lives... The other sea gives nothing. It is named The Dead Sea. There are two kinds of people in the world. There are two seas in Palestine."*[2]

Jesus lays it out very much the same way as Erwin. He says there really are two kinds of people. Some are like good sheep that know that because they have been tended to by a loving shepherd, one of their responsibilities is to serve beyond themselves. They know that with the gift of faith they have received comes the responsibility of serving deeds. And then there are goats who, like the Dead Sea, just hold on to what they have. Goats who, either deliberately or through inertia, refuse to serve are just about as useful to Christ as the Dead Sea is to its surroundings.

You know, what I learned in Lafayette was to let go and serve the people God brought my way. Oh, there were plenty of days when I did not serve—the old selfish habits always die hard. But I found that when I let go of the gifts God had given me in His service and the service of His children, then I drew closer to them and to Him. Every drop relinquished, God replaced.

I like the story of the woman who shows up just after the worship procession has headed down the center aisle of her church. When her tardiness brought her face to face with the priest who was last

2 J. John and Mark Stibbe, comp. *A Box of Delights* (London: Monarch, 2001) 178.

in the procession, she feigned ignorance and said, *"Oh, I am sorry pastor, when does the service begin?"* He smiled and whispered back, *"The service begins, when the worship is over!"*

Provoking Thought

Prayer, study of the Scriptures, worship and service are four ways that God can more effectively pour His Holy Spirit into us. As you review Jesus' list of opportunities to serve Him—is there one that really tugs at your heart? Are you called to a ministry of service to the hungry, the poor, the lonely, the imprisoned? Someone far away, someone close to home or perhaps even someone in your home? How are you called to serve?

A Prayer for Reflection

If we pray
  we will believe
If we believe
  we will love
If we love
  we will serve.
Only then can we put
  our love for God
  into living action
Through service of Christ
  in the distressing
  disguise of the Poor.

— Mother Teresa of Calcutta, d. 1997[3]

3 Kathryn Spink, comp. *In the Silence of the Heart, Meditations by Mother Teresa* (London: SPCK, 1983).

Serious Business

"Then He said to them all, 'If any want to become my followers, let them deny themselves and take up their cross daily and follow Me. For those who want to save their life will lose it, and those who lose their life for My sake will save it.'"

— Luke 9:23-24

"How seriously should one take Christianity?" I had a friend who once challenged me by saying, *"If you want to know what your priorities are, look at your calendar and your checkbook."* This is true of our relationships, and also of our allegiances. I, like many of you reading this, know people who spend far more of their time, talents and financial resources on other "non-profits" than they do on Christ's work through their church family.

This probes me to ask, *"How seriously are we to take Christianity?"* My hunch is ***very seriously.*** When Jesus began His ministry, it was mostly about calling and welcoming new followers to travel along with Him. But the longer they traveled, the more difficult the road got. And Jesus was not one to avoid transparency. Thus, as His ministry started heading toward its earthly end, He told His disciples if they continued along, it would not only get tougher, but it would get tougher *by the day. "Take up the cross daily,"* were the words Jesus used to give fair warning. Serious, serious business.

It is fairly common to make Christianity merely an intellectual exercise of debate about various views of the Almighty, or simply a social experiment wherein we tackle the societal ills of the world under the banner of Christ. But it is that serious business upon which many

modern church folk get hung up. So often faith gets stuck being lived out in my head and my body, losing its way to my heart and soul.

For instance, I can prove my intellectual stamina and my social concern. Those are fairly admirable in our world today. But to begin speaking of loving God with heart and soul may just be taking it all a bit too far. And yet that is the deep call of Christ. I once heard Former Archbishop Donald Coggan remark with great sadness, *"The journey from head to heart is one of the longest and most difficult that we know."*

My experience is that if we are indeed serious about Christianity, then we need to go deeper, rather than just know more or do more. Following Christ does not mean imitating Him, for we are not the same. Following Christ means loving Him, drawing on Him, allowing Him to enter us such that not only are minds and wills transformed, but hearts and souls as well. That is why the metaphor of "new birth," which Jesus used and to which I have already referred, is so perfect. Christ came to call us out of our selfish tendencies to a life of selfless sacrifice. It is in that place that true joy and peace are found.

Anglican theologian, Alister McGrath writes of this kind of following:

> *[Christian] Spirituality is all about the way in which we encounter and experience God, and the transformation of*

> *our consciousness and our lives as a result of that encounter and experience. It is most emphatically not the exclusive preserve of some spiritual elite, preoccupied with unhealthy perfectionist tendencies. It is the common duty and joy of all Christian believers, as they long to enter into the deeper fellowship with the living God which is promised in the Scriptures. We can think of it in terms of the internalization of our faith. It means allowing our faith to saturate every aspect of our lives, infecting and affecting our thinking, feeling, and living.*[1]

It was not merely Jesus' impact on the minds and bodies of His disciples that set them aflame with passion for God, but the transformation of hearts and souls as well. So much so that each was willing to give up life if called upon to do so.

"How seriously should one take Christianity?" I think we know. Perhaps a better question is *"How seriously do **I** take Christianity?"* To answer, you can look at your calendar and your checkbook; you can even look to your mind and your body, but perhaps the real answer rests in looking even deeper into heart and soul.

With God's help, may the journey from head to heart happen in each of us.

1 Alister McGrath, "Loving God with Heart and Mind," *Knowing and Doing,* Winter 2002.

Provoking Thought

How seriously do you take Christianity and the claims of Christ?

A Prayer for Reflection

Lord Jesus Christ,
take all my freedom,
my memory, my understanding, and my will.
All that I have and cherish
You have given me.
I surrender it all to be guided by Your will.
Your grace and Your love are wealth enough for me.
Give me these, Lord Jesus,
And I ask for nothing more.

— Prayer of Self-Dedication to
Jesus Christ from *The Roman Missal*

Whom Will You Serve?

"Now therefore revere the Lord, and serve Him in sincerity and in faithfulness; put away the gods that your ancestors served beyond the River and in Egypt, and serve the Lord. Now if you are unwilling to serve the Lord, choose this day whom you will serve, whether the gods of your ancestors served in the region beyond the River or the gods of the Amorites in whose land you are living; but as for me and my household, we will serve the Lord."

— Joshua 24:14-15

The passage comes from one of the most well-known in all of Scripture. It is one of the greatest speeches in the entire Judeo-Christian story. It is often referred to as the "Covenant Renewal at Shechem."

At this point, the long journey out of bondage in Egypt has come to its end as the faithful Hebrews are gathered. Moses' apprentice, Joshua, reminds them of their great history as a people freed from slavery, who traversed the desert for decades, who received God's Ten Commandments, and who, after such a long journey, had battled the Canaanites and were now laying claim to a land promised to them.

But the climax of his speech is not the retelling of their history, but a question: *"Now that God has seen you this far, will you go the rest of the way with Him?"* They, perhaps like you and me, had many options of who they could follow—idols, gods, personal interests and pleasures. But Joshua put it to them. The passage above says, *"Now therefore revere the Lord."* Some versions of Scripture suggest the word *"revere"* is actually more accurately translated as *"fear."* Thus, his "heads up" is, *"Before you make up your mind, fear the Lord."*

"Men who fear God face life fearlessly. Men who do not fear God end up fearing everything," wrote Richard Christian Halverson.[1] There are really two key fears when it comes to our relationship with God—fear of God and fear of everything else.

By fear of God we do not mean cowardice or anxiety before God, but "awe, honor, respect." For years, my aunt served as the Chief Justice of the Circuit Court of Appeals in the Commonwealth of Virginia. All of my life, I had known her as Aunt Jo, an easygoing, good-humored, loving mother, aunt and wife. My graduate study required that we spend three of our years in Northern Virginia, not too far from my aunt and her place of service to that great state.

One day, my wife and I decided to visit her courtroom. When we arrived, she was donned in her black robe, attorneys lined up to see her and she, literally, held court. When she spoke, everyone's attention turned to her; she was master and commander of that piece of Virginia real estate, and whether attorney, plaintiff or defendant—it was likely a good thing to fear my Aunt Jo! Unless she had complete rule, not only would the courtroom erupt into chaos, but justice itself would spin out of control.

So it goes with God. We are to fear Him, in the sense that when it comes to the real estate we call planet earth and its inhabitants, God should be the boss. Ultimately, God should have control of every single aspect of life. When He does not, things begin to fall apart, which brings me to fear two, the fear of everything else!

When we accept that all peace in our lives—the peace of the world, the peace in our home, political order, religious harmony—rests not with God, but with humankind, then we will slowly begin to descend into fear. This fear does not incorporate awe and honor, but

1 Manser 110.

anxiety. This kind of fear is the root cause of so many of our human disorders and sin. This kind of fear gives birth in us to a deep sense that there is "not enough to go around," whether that be material things (causing us to hoard or steal) or non-material things (causing us to either withhold our love or desperately seek it in wrong and harmful ways).

That is why one remedy for the second kind of fear is described in this way by John: *"There is no fear in love, but perfect love casts out fear."* [2] When we know, deep down, that we are perfectly and fully loved, then it draws out of us that sick, gnawing kind of fear. The path to that kind of freedom from fear is to fear God. John Witherspoon put it well, *"It is only the fear of God that can deliver us from the fear of man."* The real call here is to let God have His rightful place in your life as Lord and Savior personified in Christ Jesus. Then, the fears that plague our hearts and lives will melt like ice in the warm sun.

Of what are you afraid? Does it not help to know there is Someone who loves you completely, more than anyone walking the earth? That One does, indeed, deserve our fear and awe. There is comfort in that kind of love. In fact, that kind of love really does cast out fear. As good old Charles Wesley wrote: *"Jesus! The name that charms our fears; that bids our sorrows cease; 'Tis music in the sinner's ear, 'Tis life, and health, and peace!"*[3]

So, let me go back to Shechem. Perhaps Joshua should have just cut to the chase and said, *"God has carried you this far because He loves you, now think about that for a minute. You know the two choices out there, fear or God. Whom will you serve?"*

---

2 I John 4:18.
3 *The Hymnal, 1982.* (New York: The Church Hymnal Corporation, 1982) 493.

Provoking Thought

Of what are you more afraid, not being loved by God or loving God? If you know you are loved by Him, then do you still have a need to fear?

A Prayer for Reflection

At times Lord, I forget Your love for me. And, there are times I ignore it and turn from it. When I fail to receive Your love, then I find that great darkness creeping over me—with all its angst, and pain, and anxiety—all of its fear.

Help me, dear Jesus Christ, to allow You to cast aside anything that stands between Your love and me. Help me to fear You as our forebears did, so that in fearing You, I may have no fear, and at life's long end, know and receive Your perfect love.

— RJL+

Blessed is the King

"...throwing their cloaks on the colt, they set Jesus on it. As he rode along, people kept spreading their cloaks on the road. As he was now approaching the path down from the Mount of Olives, the whole multitude of the disciples began to praise God joyfully with a loud voice for all the deeds of power they had seen, saying, 'Blessed is the king who comes in the name of the Lord! Peace in heaven, and glory in the highest heaven!' Some of the Pharisees in the crowd said to Him, 'Teacher, order your disciples to stop.' He answered, 'I tell you, if these were silent, the stones would shout out.'"

— Luke 19:35-40

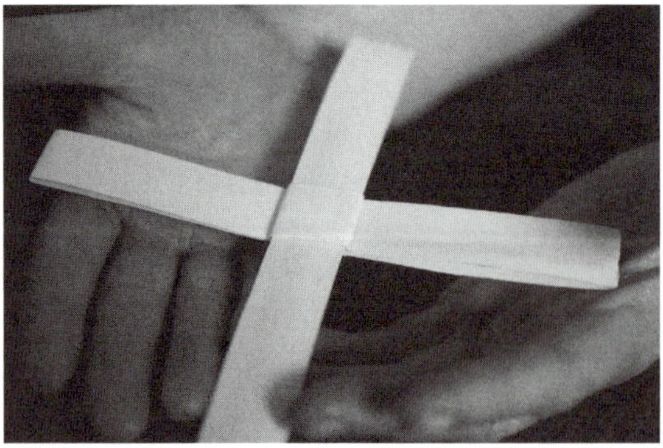

If you have been using this little book as a Lenten companion, you will have reached Holy Week—those seven days between what is known as Palm Sunday and Easter Sunday. If it is a companion for another time of year, I invite you still to consider how this week and its designation as "holy" by the traditions of our faith, still speaks today.

The little scene above is called the *Triumphal Entry,* and Matthew's Gospel adds the color green to the story by telling us it was not just

cloaks that were being flung on the ground at the hoofs of the donkey that carried Jesus, but palms being waved in the air in celebration. Despite the obvious celebration, there is a shadow over the moment when the religious leaders tell Jesus to have His followers pipe down. You can imagine Jesus with a gentle smile in return, *"You know guys, even if I told them to put a lid on it, the little stones at our feet would start to do their own chorus of praise."* But we know as the week goes on, the shadow gets longer and darker.

It is a strange turn of events in a matter of days. At the head of the week, the whole crowd is cheering Jesus, but in no time, things begin to head south. Only days later, virtually everyone who wanted to be near Jesus on that first Palm Sunday did not want to touch Him with a ten-foot pole by the time Good Friday rolled around.

What follows that *Triumphal Entry?* A few more salient teachings, healings, and then betrayal, trial, torture, crucifixion. We probably would like to really bypass all of this and go straight to the good news of Easter Sunday, but you just cannot have a resurrection without a death. In the next few meditations, we will explore different aspects of holiness and Holy Week.

Perhaps one of the most famous of Palm Sunday hymns is one entitled, *All Glory Laud and Honor.* The story goes that when Charlemagne died, his son, Louis I, assumed the throne of his mighty father. All went well until he began to divide the massive kingdom, and then it all began to fall apart. He never enjoyed the security of the throne his father had. Caught in the middle of all of this was Theodulph, Bishop of Orleans, a city in the south of France. He was an incredible leader who worked hard to reform the clergy, establish schools, advance education and build churches. Advocating high morals, he was a brilliant man who also composed hymns. But, during the intrigues of Louis' reign, he was falsely accused of siding against his monarch and imprisoned on Easter Sunday.

Tradition says that Louis later visited the place of Theodulph's imprisonment and halted outside the Bishop's window, who in return sang this well-known hymn that he, himself, wrote while in that prison. It is said that the king was so moved that he immediately ordered the Bishop's release.

Originally, there were seventy-eight verses to the hymn! Rarely are all of them sung today, but they are a reminder of how very dark things do not always have the last word. What faith he must have had to write these words in the darkness of a prison! *"All glory, laud, and honor, To Thee, Redeemer King, To whom the lips of children, Made sweet hosannas ring."* Somehow the acknowledgement of those first Hosannas to our King's trek toward Good Friday, in the end, meant release for the Bishop. So it can for each of us as well.

So, let us begin our descent toward the Cross with Bishop Theodulph's hymn; let us even travel to the darkness of his cell and ponder our own Lord's descent. Let us hold in our hearts the promises that in keeping our eyes fixed on Christ, there will be sweet release in the story's end, or perhaps, beginning.

Provoking Thought

Some define the word holy as meaning "set apart." What is holy to you? If the days ahead are to be treated as a "holy week," what can you do to personally make it set apart from all other weeks?

A Prayer for Reflection

Dear Master, we remember that many who claimed you as King on Sunday shouted "crucify" on Friday. So confirm our faith today that our love for you will never falter or turn to hatred but will remain constant now and forever. We offer our worship to you, Lord, with all our love. Amen.[1]

1 Hazel Snashall, comp. *Prayers before Worship* (Lawrenceville: National Christian Education Council, 1984).

Dealing With the Cover-up

"Then the eyes of both were opened, and they knew that they were naked; and they sewed fig leaves together and made loincloths for themselves. They heard the sound of the Lord God walking in the garden at the time of the evening breeze, and the man and his wife hid themselves from the presence of the Lord God among the trees of the garden."

— Genesis 3:7-8

We opened this little journey talking a good bit about death and sin, and we are going to circle back as we head toward a conclusion. It is true that when God created all the wonderful pieces of the earth, He ended His majestic project by looking on it and saying, *"It is very good."*[1]

The truth that springs from the story of the Garden of Eden is important. God set humankind free, but warned them that disobedience carried the price of sin and death. All was good and well, but somewhere

1 Genesis 1:31.

along the line, Adam and Eve spent too much time with the serpent. They ate, they fell, sin entered and it all came unraveled. The good turned sour.

Whenever the above passage is read in church, I usually encounter a member who just has to comment, perhaps with a little grin, on that "naked" business. The grin is there I suppose, to hide the bit of discomfort we may feel thinking about the first humans out there in the Garden without a stitch on. What was going on here?

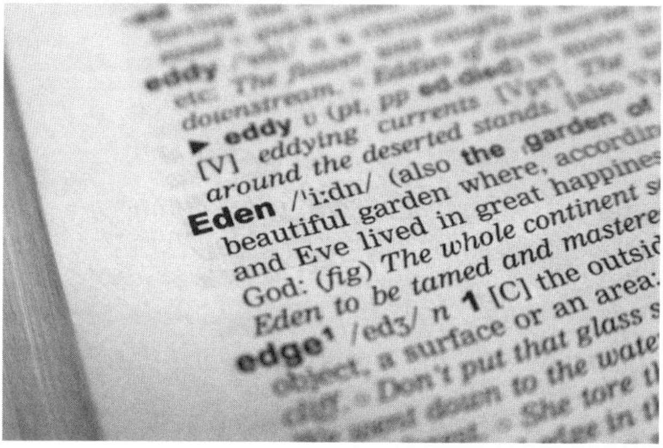

Adam and Eve *knew* they had done something wrong in the same way a child quickly snaps his hand out of the cookie jar and begins whistling when Mom enters the room as an attempt to divert her attention. Adam and Eve were dealing with their own guilt by drawing attention away from who they were created to be (naked, pure, innocent) to the new fallen creatures (red-faced, caught, shamed).

God left that curse of covering nakedness as a kind of reminder that we always should be, *with His help,* working back toward our innocence and nakedness.

Several years ago, I was fortunate to spend some time in Japan. I will be honest and say my Japanese was pretty much limited to key words like, "Please," "Thank you," "Excuse me" and "Which way to the bathroom?" I have learned that the Japanese have two words to describe how humans present themselves to the world. The first is *tatemae'* or "the part of myself that I let the world see," and *hon ne,* "that place on the inside where no one can see." Philip Yancey suggests that perhaps we need a third word for the secret places that we never make known to anyone.

I am suggesting to you that it is the third place that God is trying to get to, open up, heal and make known. God really wants more than just the faces we give to the world, but also the one that we try to hide from Him. Yancey confesses, *"In vain I sometimes build barriers to keep God out, stubbornly disregarding the fact that God looks on the heart, penetrating beyond the tatemae and hon ne to where no person can see. As God informed the prophet Samuel, 'The Lord does not look at the things man looks at. Man looks at the outward appearance, but the Lord looks at the heart.'"*[2]

As my mentor John Stott likes to say, *"What happened in the Garden, was the first instance of a 'cover-up!'"* I wonder what would have happened if rather than reach for the fig leaves, Adam and Eve just 'fessed up, waited in the Garden and when God returned, admitted in all their nakedness and shame what had happened? Surely, in some sense, they would have restored a real honesty with God about who they were and about how much they needed God not just when everything was good, but also when things went terribly wrong.

We need this too, you know. The journey between Palm Sunday and Easter Sunday is a good season to lay bare before God what is going on inside. If we strip away the clothes of pretense before God, perhaps even before others, we can really be available to one another and, of course, to God.

There is much in today's world to give others the impression that we are so superbly self-sufficient. But often, only you and God know what is going on behind closed doors.

But when one strips off the outer shell, the "clothes" if you will, that is when real intimacy and authentic love can take place. Perhaps pause, take some time to be honest with God; do not let Him just see your game face, but all your faces. Invite Him into not just your public garden, but the private one as well. Let Him show you where the weeds are, where new growth is needed, what needs to be pruned and what needs to be tended.

My thought is if you do you will find yourself, come Easter morning, emerging from whatever tomb you may face today.

---

2 Yancey 46; I Samuel 16:7.

Provoking Thought

What is one thing you are hiding (or think you are hiding) from God right now that really needs to be laid bare before Him?

A Prayer for Reflection

O Lord, I have sinn'd, and the black number swells
To such a dismal sum,
That should my stony heart and eyes,
And this whole sinful trunk a flood become,
And melt to tears, their drops could not suffice
To count my score,
Much less to pay
But thou, my God, hast blood in store,
Yet, since the balsam of thy blood,
Although it can, will do no good,
Unless the wound be cleans'd in tears before;
Thou in whose sweet, but pensive face,
Laughter could never steal a place,
Teach but my heart and eyes
To melt away,
And then one drop of balsam will suffice.

— Jeremy Taylor, d. 1667
Bishop of Down and Connor
Vice-Chancellor of Dublin University[3]

3 Counsell 276-277.

The Black Bean

"...He has appeared once for all at the end of the age to remove sin by the sacrifice of himself. And just as it is appointed for mortals to die once, and after that the judgment, so Christ, having been offered once to bear the sins of many, will appear a second time, not to deal with sin, but to save those who are eagerly waiting for Him."

— Hebrews 9:26-28

It was not just shame and guilt that grew out of the disobedience of those first humans, but death as well. God's intent was that life would reign. But with sin, death came into the picture, along with things like decay and rust. And as much as we wince at the thought, each of us has been grafted into the family that must face a last day.

My wife and I are Texans now. Any good Texan soon learns he or she has to make a kind of Lone Star pilgrimage to *The Alamo,* which we did within weeks of our move across the state's border. The trip to this place, a kind of nexus point of history and tragedy was humbling and disquieting. It reminded me of my first trip to the USS Arizona's "remains" in Pearl Harbor nearly four decades ago.

Most know the battle cry, "Remember the Alamo," and the very dark events that surrounded those hallowed grounds were, in a very real way, a kind of tangible fertilizer that empowered the people of the future Texas to eventually defeat Santa Anna at the Battle of San Jacinto on April 21, 1836. The same could be said of Pearl Harbor. That day of infamy was a turning point that not only called for a response, but demanded it. In the end, it was probably reflecting on that day that continued to empower the men and women of our Armed Forces to

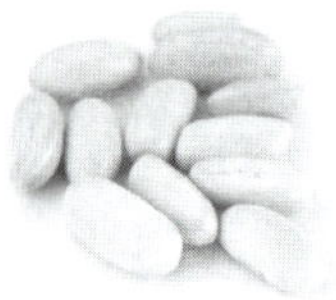

defeat the enemies that had attacked us. Strange how something dark, even ominous, can in some way be redeemed.

My wife and I took notice of one of Santa Anna's terrifying methods of executing his prisoners, the "Black Bean." May 14, 1836 marked the day of Texas' independence from Mexico. The Mexican government had forced Santa Anna into retirement because of his great defeat. This did not last long when over disputes with the French, Santa Anna emerged from retirement in 1839. A mere two years later, Santa Anna was once again president with dictator power. In October of 1841, Santa Anna ordered Texas prisoners to be marched back to Mexico. Countless prisoners died along the way; a tally of the dead was kept by stringing their ears on a leather thong. San Antonio was invaded by Santa Anna's Mexican Army in 1842, and in retaliation the Texans seized the town of Mier only to immediately surrender it. During the march to Mexico, the prisoners revolted and escaped only to be recaptured.

As punishment for the attempted escape, Santa Anna decided to execute one man for every ten men that would live. Each man was blindfolded and forced to draw a bean from a bag. A white bean meant the prisoner lived and went back to the jail. However, if a black bean was drawn the prisoner was executed by firing squad.

There is a black bean at the Alamo with the appropriate write-up and a letter that one young man wrote to his mother after he had drawn one of Santa Anna's black beans. It was daunting indeed to read the young fellow's words of dread, of knowing his death was only moments away. But then, he did hope that his death would bring meaning to his life.

We are days away from contemplating the day our Lord drew a black bean. It is a vivid reminder that someday, each one of us will draw ours as well. There is a connection we need to make here. The passage from Hebrews begins to lay out that connection for us.

Now how can we—in much the same way survivors of the Alamo or Pearl Harbor did—turn this black bean reminder into something that defeats the darkness? Here is a good reason to spend some time thinking about death. If you know it is coming, then what are you doing with your life? What are you allowing Jesus Christ to do with your life to help you prepare for that moment? How are you living? How are you preparing to die? Are you prepared for what comes after death? These are ***very important questions*** that we should be asking.

I would have hated to have been one of those prisoners who reached in Santa Anna's "bean bag," but then I know I already have. We have all drawn the black bean and there is no getting around that. The question is, are we prepared for what comes with that? Better yet, are you allowing God to help you prepare for what comes with that?

Provoking Thought

Knowing that you have drawn the black bean, what are you doing to prepare for that moment? And for what follows?

A Prayer for Reflection

God is eternal light.
May I die at peace with my God.
Lord, stay by our door.

— An Early Christian inscription[1]

1 Adalbert-G. Hamman, comp. *Early Christian Prayers* (Chicago: H. Regnery Co., 1961).

Doubt-Proof

"Now faith is the assurance of things hoped for, the conviction of things not seen. Indeed, by faith our ancestors received approval. By faith we understand that the worlds were prepared by the word of God, so that what is seen was made from things that are not visible."

— Hebrews 11:1-3

"Do you think people ever doubt that God exists?" This was the question of one of my pre-adolescent children, as we stood in line, waiting outside of a barbeque joint near the parish I was serving on the Gulf Coast of Florida. Actually, when the question popped out, I was thinking about something that was kind of weighing me down. And yet here one of those "little children" that Jesus was so fond of, was thinking on even weightier matters than I![1] It was, however, a good, honest question that helped me get out of my mood!

I have, in the course of my service, often had that question put to me more by the grown-ups than the youngsters. And of course the answer is "Yes." I think at times, perhaps the underlying question is often, *"Is it okay to doubt the existence of God?"* My answer is usually only slightly squishy, *"It may not be okay, but it is quite normal!"*

Whenever I do get this question, I realize it usually means the one with the query is not running away from God, but towards Him; they are on a search. They have opened their minds and hearts to begin really exploring faith.

Peter, at least in this stage of my middle-aged life, is probably my favorite of the Apostles. The poor and wonderful Peter had it right

1 Matthew 19:14, Mark 10:14, Luke 18:16.

and wrong more than all the others combined. One minute he was confessing Christ, the next minute confused about Christ; one minute walking on water, the next minute sinking; one minute pledging his loyalty to Christ, the next minute denying the same.[2] And, of all things mystifying, it was upon this shaky person, whom Jesus would nickname "The Rock," that Jesus chose to build the church.[3]

We are told that by the time Jesus' body was growing cold in the tomb, virtually all of the Apostles had given up hope. They had three of the best years of seminary education anyone could hope for. They had actually been with Jesus, seen the miracles, heard the words, felt His touch! And yet, by the time the nails were being pulled from the dead flesh, doubt had consumed them and they turned and walked away.

It is certain that much of what we know in Christianity seems worthy of thoughtful skepticism. But is that all bad? I remember a line that has been of help to me over the years from Mary Shelley's *Frankenstein, "Without doubt there would be no need for faith."*

It is *faith* that gets us through the doubts. Doubts are normal. Alongside the Apostles, we are in good company. But at some point we might want to remember Jesus' gentle, loving, though clear reprimand to the most famous doubter, Thomas, *"Stop doubting and believe!"*[4]

The passage from Hebrews on the previous page is known as the "Great Faith Chapter" of the Bible because it retells the incredible, miraculous story of God working with His followers over the centuries and how faith played a key role in each case. But faith, like all good things from God, is a gift. It cannot be bought or earned, only received. There are many things that may block our faith—our reason, intellect, reluctance to be seen as one foolish enough to embrace

2 Matthew 16:13-28; 14:22-35; John 13 and 18.
3 Matthew 16:18.
4 John 20:27.

things that cannot be proven, fear of placing trust in something that may ultimately not be true, and yes, even our doubt. If we could but empty ourselves of all those various things that clog our spiritual arteries, faith will find its way into our spiritual circulation. What we once doubted, we can embrace as truth.

In the last few days of this daily reader, we will be looking at the primary foci of the entire Christian Gospel, and much of what we are told cannot really be "proven" in a way that we might prove where the first President lived. But we are ultimately not called to live by proof, but as both the Old and New Testaments remind us, *"The righteous live by faith."*[5]

"Do people ever doubt the existence of God?" Well, yes, of course... I have. "Is it *okay?"* Such doubt is normal; it is something with which we all struggle, but ultimately, we are called to a place of faith. How does one have such faith? Know that God wishes to give it. It is a gift. Pray for it. Make sure the stuff that gets in the way of faith is tossed aside. Give yourself the gift of believing in all those wonderful truths shared by the Judeo-Christian story.

The rather well-known Christian apologist, John McDowell, puts it this way:

> *The most telling testimony of all must be the lives of those early Christians. We must ask ourselves: What caused them to go everywhere telling the message of the risen Christ?*
>
> *Had there been any visible benefits accruing to them from their efforts—prestige, wealth, increased social status or material benefits—we might logically attempt to account for their actions, for their wholehearted and total allegiance to this 'risen Christ.'*
>
> *As a reward for their efforts, however, those early Christians were beaten, stoned to death, thrown to the lions, tortured, crucified. Every conceivable method was used to stop them from talking.*
>
> *Yes, they were peaceful people. They forced their beliefs on no one. Rather, they laid down their lives as the ultimate proof of their complete confidence in the truth of their message.*
>
> *It has been rightly said that they went through the test of death to determine their veracity. It is important to remember*

5 Habakkuk 2:4; Galatians 3:11.

that initially the disciples didn't believe.

But once convinced—in spite of their doubts—they were never to doubt again that Christ was raised from the dead.[6]

It would be great if there was some pill we could take, some exercise we could do, some magic mantra we could say that would somehow doubt-proof our journey through the Christian faith. Unfortunately, there is not. But there is one thing that might aid us. It springs from a little scene in Mark's Gospel and it is as much comical as it is profound.

Jesus has just finished saying, *"If you are able! All things can be done for the one who believes."* And someone immediately jumps up and says, *"I believe;* ***help my unbelief!"***[7] See, even the believer needed a little help believing. Maybe that cry *"help my unbelief,"* is a good place to start when you are looking for something that is doubt-proof.

Provoking Thought

What is there in the telling of Christianity that you doubt? Why? And if you did believe, what difference might it make in your life?

A Prayer for Reflection

Give us, O Lord, a steadfast heart, which no unworthy affection may drag downwards; give us an unconquered heart, which no tribulation can wear out; give us an upright heart, which no unworthy purpose may tempt aside. Bestow upon us also, O Lord our God, understanding to know you, diligence to seek you, wisdom to find you and a faithfulness that may finally embrace you; through Jesus Christ our Lord.

— St. Thomas Aquinas, d. 1274[8]

6 Josh McDowell, *Christianity: Hoax or History?* (Carol Stream: Tyndale House, 1998).
7 Mark 9:23-24.
8 Counsell 137.

Something New

"I give you a new commandment, that you love one another. Just as I have loved you, you also should love one another. By this everyone will know that you are my disciples, if you have love for one another."

— John 13:34-35

It is kind of hard to wiggle out of or around Jesus' direct commandment for us to *"love one another."* The Latin phrase used for this poignant moment in the telling of Jesus' last hours on earth is *mandatum novum,* literally translated, new command. It is the story most churches in Christendom tell on Maundy Thursday.

Now you may think one of the Apostles might have piped up and said, *"Um... Jesus, don't we have enough commands? I mean really. The Ten Commandments are hard enough, but here You go adding an eleventh!"* But of course, Jesus' point was to promote the most important commandment. You can obey all of the "Big Ten" and still not "love one another." And perhaps the only real way to obey is to allow the commandments to grow out of love for the other.

Whenever I officiate at a wedding, I take notice that the response of the couple in the liturgy that I use is not "I do," but "I will." What is the difference? "I do," usually implies, "I always will." But is that possible? Many of the couples I marry have broken some part of their vows to love, honor and cherish before the wedding reception is over!

A realistic hope is not that perfection will exist, but the "will" to get to that place of perfection is always there. Thus, "I will" is possible, "I do," really is not. Why?

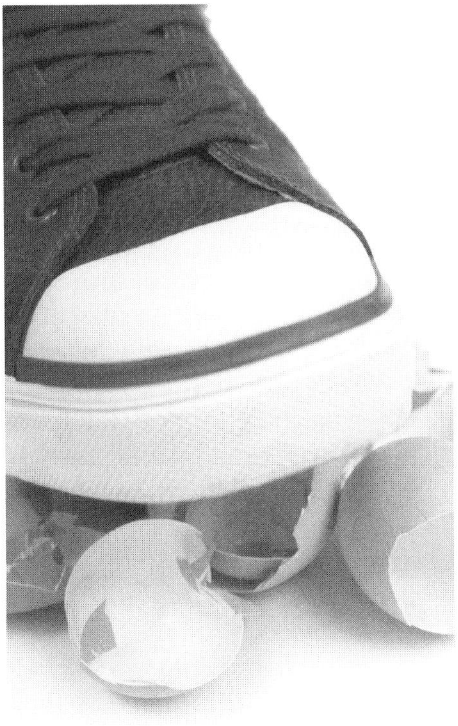

What if, in marriage, friendship and family ties, the relationship depended upon what you did, rather than who you were and what you meant to the other? Would it not mean a lifetime of walking on eggshells? Healthy relationships are not grounded in an unrealistic expectation of perfection, but a love of the other, with the hope that love will bear the fruit of right actions. In short, a wedding does not a marriage make; it is a loving commitment in the presence of God that makes the marriage. The fruit of that love will be loving actions toward the other. The same is true of any relationship and perhaps that is what Jesus was trying to knock into the heads of those Apostles before He began His journey toward the Cross.

Christianity begins with relationship. God loves us because of who we are, not what we do. God's love is that of a parent toward a child. Our peace, life and salvation in this life and the life to come is not dependent on our end of the equation. It is found on God's end, God's initiative, God's mercy. Our only appropriate response can be, like grace and faith, to receive.

There is an interesting line in the book of Hebrews that may speak to this tension between how we live, love and obey all at the same time. The author writes, *"For by a single offering He has perfected for all time those who are sanctified."*[1] This lays out the interesting paradox of the "one sacrifice" which is of course the death of our Lord on the Cross for *"the sins of the whole world."*[2] It is our embrace of that price paid on our behalf that makes us perfect in God's eyes. Jesus is the lens through which God sees us. But notice, as the Hebrews passage acknowledges, while Jesus *"has perfected"* (a compound verb that describes a condition—here, perfection) His followers, they are also

1 Hebrews 10:14.
2 John 1:29.

being *"sanctified"* (a compound verb that describes a process—here, sanctification, or the process of being made holy).

Thus, perfect indeed, but at the same time in the process, a kind of ongoing work, of being made holy. We are in this relationship with God not because of what we do, but who we are, objects of God's love. That love, in return, brings about our obedience and so on. So a Christian's morality begins with relationship... an embrace of God's love, which grows within us a love that embraces the other. *"By this others will know you are with Me,"* Jesus said, *"That you love each other."* Perhaps it was another way of saying, *"You can obey all the commandments you want, but if you do not love each other then what difference does obedience make?"*

As with marriages and friendships, depth often determines strength and breadth. I thank God my wife does not demand my perfection as a price for the love she gives. If she did, I would not make the cut! Thank God, He does not demand my perfection as a price for the love He gives—I would not make that cut either. Instead, God's love given should awaken a desire to love in return. With God's help, and with that awakening, one can begin the process toward not only being the husband, wife, friend or child one should, but the Christian as well.

So what Jesus offered on that first Maundy Thursday was something new. Of course, He had been saying it in lots of ways over a number of years in so many places, but the message had not been given that way before. The choosing of this night, this moment, must have meant it was very, very important. Again, *"love one another."* Something new.

Provoking Thought

How do you experience God's love? How do you share it?

A Prayer for Reflection

My God, I desire to love thee perfectly, with all my heart which thou madest for thyself, with all my mind which only thou canst satisfy, with all my soul which fain would soar to thee, with all my strength, my feeble strength, which shrinks before so great a task, and yet can choose naught else but spend itself in loving thee. Claim thou my heart, fill thou my mind, uplift my soul, and reinforce my strength, that where I fail thou mayest succeed in me, and make me love thee perfectly.

— Father Walter Howard Frere, d. 1938[3]

3 Counsell 400.

The Two Sides of the Cross

"So they took Jesus; and carrying the cross by himself, He went out to what is called The Place of the Skull, which in Hebrew is called Golgotha. There they crucified Him..."

—John 19:16-18

One should perhaps read all of the Passion narrative we find unfolding between Maundy Thursday until that moment when the stone closes Jesus' grave. There are reflections aplenty, and even more books that look at the Cross event from all sides. I have certainly brushed up against it in various places here in this companion you have been reading.

One way of understanding the Cross of Christ is to embrace the truth that there are "two sides." While we always, to some degree, live in some sort of tension between these two sides, they spring to life a bit more during any season of serious reflection. What are the two sides? The Good Friday side of the Cross and the Easter side of the Cross.

Everything that rests before Easter is obviously the Good Friday side. It is here that we meet with those broken areas of our lives: temptations, sins, darkness or as a friend of mine likes to say, the "attachments" that need to be released. On this side of the Cross there is judgment and we have to come to terms with that. Romans 3:23 says it quite clearly, *"all have sinned and fall short of the glory of God."* All means *all,* not some, or a few, or even most, but all. What put Jesus up on that Cross was not an angry mob, an upset religious establishment or Roman soldiers doing their job—it was sin, yours, mine and ours. So as we stand on this side, the feeling is mighty morose and there should be bubbling up within us a deep desire to be rid of all this mess. So here we come to terms with it all—we confess that darkness, we hand it over and with the grace of God we repent and start life anew.

Then, thank God there is the Easter side of the Cross which promises forgiveness, redemption and salvation both here and in the life eternal. That forgiveness is freely given as none of us was actually

there when Jesus was nailed to the Cross. None of us was there when He made the decision to willingly give Himself as a ransom for all people everywhere for all time.[1] That is the Easter message, but we do not have to live on the Good Friday side of the Cross either. With the help of God's grace, we can step from that darkness into the light of resurrection. A resurrection life creeps out here from time to time, but it is really preparing us for a life eternal.

Dietrich Bonhoeffer, a German Lutheran pastor, was executed at an early age by the Nazis only a day or so before his prison was liberated by the allies. He did more in less than four decades than most could do in four lifetimes. Clearly, he had seen both sides of the Cross. Perhaps that is why he wrote, *"Only as someone judged by God can a human being live before God... In the form of the Crucified we recognize and find ourselves. Accepted by God, judged and reconciled in the cross: That is the reality of humankind."*[2]

Spend some time with the Cross today, perhaps tomorrow as well. By that, I do not mean spend more time bowing as it passes or crossing yourself, but spend time ***with the Cross.*** Allow it to judge you. It tells us where the sickness is and where we need the medicine of Christ. When we get a grip on that, then perhaps we can fully appreciate, and receive its Easter side.

1 Mark 10:45; I Timothy 2:6; Hebrews 9:15.
2 Dietrich Bonhoeffer, *Meditations on the Cross* (Louisville: Westminster John Knox, 1998) 51.

Provoking Thought

Close your eyes for a few moments and meditate on the image of the Cross of Christ. What thoughts, feelings, words or prayers come to mind?

A Prayer for Reflection

Forgive them all, O Lord; our sins of omission and our sins of commission; the sins of our youth and the sins of our riper years; the sins of our souls and the sins of our bodies; our secret and our more open sins; our sins of ignorance and surprise, and our more deliberate and presumptuous sins; the sins we have done to please others; the sins we know and remember, and the sins we have forgotten; the sins we have striven to hide from others and the sins by which we have made others offend; forgive them, O Lord, forgive them all for his sake, who died for our sins and rose for our justification, and now stands at the right hand to make intercession for us, Jesus Christ our Lord. Amen.

Jesus, poor, unknown and despised, have mercy on us, and let us not be ashamed to follow you. Jesus, accused, and wrongfully condemned, teach us to bear insults patiently, and let us not seek our own glory. Jesus, crowned with thorns and hailed in derision; buffeted, overwhelmed with injuries, grief and humiliations; Jesus, hanging on the accursed tree, bowing the head, giving up the ghost, have mercy on us, and conform our whole lives to your spirit. Amen.

— John Wesley, d. 1791[3]

3 Counsell 314.

Save Us

"But as for me, I will look to the Lord, I will wait for the God of my salvation; my God will hear me."

— Micah 7:7

Micah, like all Old Testament prophets, had but one real mission: to try to call God's people back to a relationship with Him; to not only see, but embrace God as the source of all comfort, hope, peace and salvation; to avert their eyes, minds and hearts away from competing gods, forces and powers; and to cause reconciliation between Creator and created.

The culmination of the prophet's work is fulfilled in the life, death and resurrection of Jesus. But one does not get to Easter Sunday without moving through Good Friday and Holy Saturday. We need to maintain, even as our eyes strain for sunrise on Easter morn, what Lord George Carey calls a "cross spirituality." He writes that such spirituality calls on us to embrace that the Christian is already dead and yet alive in Christ. If that is the case, then the Christian must embrace the Cross with full force. In his words:

> *I must try to live under the cross daily. I must put my Savior always before me as my example, friend, and guide. I must live a life that pleases him. The problem is that it is hard. A friend*

> *once remarked: 'We are expected to be living sacrifices, but the problem is we keep crawling off the altar.' How right he was! How necessary it is for each one of us to apply the cross to our daily lives—to our giving to one another and to God... Skin deep Christianity will not endure, but heart Christianity will, because it is marked with a cross.*[1]

While there are few references in Holy Scripture, the historic statements of faith of the Apostles Creed of the 2nd century, the Nicene Creed of the 4th century and the Creed of St. Athanasius of the late 5th or early 6th century all tell us that after His death, Jesus Christ descended into hell.[2] The assumption is that the journey between Good Friday and Easter Sunday, for Jesus, ran right through the depth of all creation, a place of utter abandonment from God's presence that surely Jesus felt descending upon Him when He cried out from the Cross, *"My God, my God, why have you forsaken me?"*[3]

But this descent was certainly part of Jesus' taking our place for our sins. This descent was His most precious act of love in trying to, like the prophets of old, bring God's people back to Him. This pause in the story is a horrific silence that finally must bring utter humility before what Christ is doing in our stead.

I wrote earlier about my time of service on the Gulf Coast. It was, in many ways, a wonderful season of my life and ministry among loving and active Christians. Only a short drive from white beaches and crystal clear waters, hardly a day went by when I was not able to behold the hand of God in the beauty of His creation. However, sometimes the beauty could turn wicked, and that is precisely what happened in September of 2004.

The waters off of Africa produced one of the largest hurricanes in recorded history—Ivan. It grew to the size of Texas and slammed into Pensacola, Florida as a strong Category III storm. The worst of

1 Carey 125.
2 Matthew 12:40; Ephesians 4:9-10; I Peter 3:19.
3 Matthew 27:46.

the storm lasted nearly twelve hours. When it was over, more than 25,000 homes were either destroyed or sustained major damage. Hundreds of businesses were affected, several people were killed and many others injured.

For all kinds of reasons, my wife and I decided to ride the storm out in our home with our three children. Sometime in the night, we began to feel we had made a terrible decision. The winds just outside our doors were literally howling. News reports a few days later would tell that dozens of tornadoes skipped down through the area from the sky and wreaked havoc as far as the eye could see. We lived a short walk from Escambia Bay where the winds forced water, which had no place to go, into a fifty-foot tidal wave that tore the Interstate Highway 10 bridge in half. Winds kept moving until virtually all the homes on the eastern shore of the bay were destroyed. All of this was going on while we were huddled in one room of our house with a small kerosene lamp.

About 2:00 AM, the winds clearly had reached their worst. We could hear the crash of trees and limbs falling on every side of the house. The plywood we had used to cover our windows was either beginning to blow off, or flap like playing cards. It was then that my bride went and got out one of our family prayer books.

She turned to a service that had often brought us comfort in times of incredible distress, Compline.

"The Lord Almighty grant us a peaceful night and a perfect end. Amen," we prayed together. Would it be the end? We did not know.

A confession of sin and then words we repeated again and again until dawn's early light, *"O God, make speed to save us. O Lord, make haste to help us."*[4] We could only, at that moment, hold fast to the One Micah preached was *"the God of my salvation."*

Nothing else would give us peace on that night—not money, health, even our home—nothing. We finally had to put all that we were and would be in His hands. And when dawn came, we emerged from our home. It looked like a giant had walked in a circle around our house the night before, trees literally encircled the home.

I am not one who believes God saves this house or that person because He plays favorites. It did not matter how we got through the night, nor did it really matter what went on outside our doors. What

4 *The Book of Common Prayer* 128.

mattered was that the only real eye of the storm was holding fast to one another and to God. It was a long, long night, but dawn came again and we were safe and saved.

The journey between Good Friday and Easter Sunday was a long, long night. In that season of spiritual pregnancy, one can do nothing but wait for what rests with the first sunrise of a world that would soon know Resurrection. And holding on to that alone will not only make us safe, but will also save us.

Provoking Thought

Think on a "Holy Saturday" in your life. How did you wait that season out? Where did you encounter the peace of God?

A Prayer for Reflection

Our darkness is never darkness in your sight;
The deepest night is clear as the daylight.

Stay with me, remain here with me,
Watch and pray, watch and pray.

Wait for the Lord, whose day is near.
Wait for the Lord: keep watch, take heart!

Within our darkest night, you kindle the fire
That never dies away, that never dies away.

— A prayer of the Taizé Community

The Way... Out

"The women were terrified and bowed their faces to the ground, but the men said to them, 'Why do you look for the living among the dead? He is not here, but has risen.'"

— Luke 24:5

One of my closest friends and most trusted advisors is a recovering alcoholic and former cocaine and gambling addict. He used to tell me that for many of his young adult years, he was in the grip of this "triple-threat." Through the help of friends, a community of faith and trust in God, he escaped their clutches, recovered and went on to live a life that no one, not even he, could have imagined when he was in his darkest moments. So, in my pastoral work when I encounter someone with similar addictions, while I would pray with them and offer what spiritual comfort I could, often my next step was to put them in touch with my friend. Why? *Because he had been where they were and could help show them the way out.*

If you have traveled the journey of this book from the first page to this one, we have been reflecting on several views of the Christian story through the prism of a God who wants to be in a relationship with us—so much so that He finally came in human form. To quote Lord Carey once more, *"Here is a Messiah who by becoming one of us knows all about human weakness, about human life and development. He knows all about sadness, temptation and the grubby facts of life. I can take comfort in this, knowing that my Lord has entered into our humanity and brought it home to God."*[1]

It was this same Messiah who was able to survive betrayal, torture, execution, even hell itself. When it was all over, Jesus stepped from the

1 Carey 104.

grave to show that God's power was, and is, greater than any darkness of which we humans can dream. That is why, when all is said and done, it is so important that we who bear the name Christian turn to Christ. *He has been where we will go and can help show us the way out.*

We began this journey with that stark reminder, *"Remember you are dust, and to dust you shall return."* Those words are supposed to remind us of our deaths and the sin that causes them. Death was not God's original plan; we started all of that by turning from God to self. Once that happened, there was no turning back—sin infected humanity, and still does today.

Thank God, He loved us so much that He could not just leave us in our sin and death, but sent His Son Christ into the world to save sinners like you and me.[2] Love compelled God to share creation with us and love compelled God to come, in the person of Christ to live among us, so that new life might be restored where it had been corrupted. As my mentor John Claypool used to say to me, *"Remember, the last things are not the worst things."* How to face those last things? Turn to Christ, and lo and behold, we encounter the "expert" not just in survival, but resurrection. Take His hand and hear His words, *"Peace be with you,"* as He steps from the grave, and we will come to know not just the possibility, but the reality of Resurrection.

When I was young, one of my favorite movies was Audie Murphy's *To Hell and Back*, which told the actor's own incredible story of defeating virtually an army of Nazi soldiers on his own. A few years back, I visited his grave at Arlington National Cemetery, and I remember goose bumps appearing on my arms, as I stood so close to the remains of a man who had faced death up close and personal, and yet had survived.

---

2 I Timothy 1:15.

Now our story says that Jesus *really did go* "to hell and back," but His remains are nowhere to be found. *Why?* Because for Jesus, death was not the last word. So Jesus responds to our betrayal with forgiveness, to our torture with endurance, to our execution with submission, to death with commendation and to hell with embrace. But when it is all over, Jesus pronounces victory over each. He has been there, lived through it all and finally conquered it all.

I suppose some people might have questioned my trust in a friend who had lived in so many dark places. I did not because I knew him and also knew him to be trustworthy. I felt it was worth the risk. And I suppose some people might question my giving my life and life's work to One who claimed to make it "to hell and back." But I do not, because I have come to know Him as best as my faculties and faith will allow, and I have found Him to be trustworthy. And I feel it is worth the risk.

But then is it a risk? Not really. I love this little scene from Luke's Gospel when the women find the tomb empty. At first, they are terrified, but then the words, *"Why do you look for the living among the dead? He is not here, He is risen."* Wow! Those are good words for any who face darkness in their lives. And they are even better words for all of us who might find the idea of death just a bit daunting, if not terrifying. Why?

Because He has been where we will go and if we turn to Him, He will show us the way out. Well?

Provoking Thought

What does the promise of Easter mean for the empty tombs of your life? And what does it mean for you as we all face the door of death?

A Prayer for Reflection

Most Glorious Lord of Life! That, on this day,
Didst make thy triumph over death and sin;
And, having harrowed hell, didst bring away
Captivity thence captive, us to win:
This joyous day, dear Lord, with joy begin;
And grant that we, for whom thou didst die,
Being with thy dear blood clean washed from sin,
May live forever in felicity!
And that thy love we weighing worthily,
May likewise love thee for the same again;
And for thy sake, that all like dear didst buy,
With love may one another entertain!
So let us love, dear Love, like as we ought,
Love is the lesson which the Lord us taught.

— Edmund Spenser, d. 1599[3]

3 Counsell 226-227.

Well?

"Now when Jesus came into the district of Caesarea Philippi, he asked his disciples, 'Who do people say that the Son of Man is?' And they said, 'Some say John the Baptist, but others Elijah, and still others Jeremiah or one of the prophets.' He said to them, 'But who do you say that I am?' Simon Peter answered, 'You are the Messiah, the Son of the living God.' And Jesus answered him, 'Blessed are you, Simon son of Jonah! For flesh and blood has not revealed this to you, but my Father in heaven.'"

— Matthew 16:13-17

On a few of the meditations I have offered you, my reader, I have concluded with the word *"Well?"* I confess that I picked that up from my mentor of nearly twenty years, until his untimely death, John Claypool. John often ended his sermon with that probing word, hoping that someone out there hearing him might take his words past ears and head to heart and soul.

Let me 'fess up a bit here. The underlying agenda of this work is not only to offer Scripture passages, various insights, provoking thoughts and prayers about a life in Christ Jesus, but also to provide you an opportunity to step more deeply into that life, and perhaps for some, for the very first time.

The Confession of Peter, which we read about in Matthew's Gospel above, was a key moment in the life and ministry of Jesus. Caesarea Philippi was actually a rather pagan city with lots of competing philosophies, religions, preachers and prophets. Perhaps it was for this reason, this moment and in this city that Jesus chose to ask the Apostles the most important question of His time. *"Who do people say that I am?"*

It was not that He did not know—it was that He wanted to see if *they knew.* Did these, the closest twelve who would carry the message forward, did they "get it?" At first, clearly most did not. They begin to pitch out answers like junior high school children who are scrambling to answer the teacher's question when no one has studied the material.

Then Jesus zooms in on Peter, *"But what about you, who do you say that I am?"* Peter takes a deep breath, and then names it, hits the nail on the proverbial head, *"You are the Messiah, the Son of the living God."* And Jesus says, *"Blessed are you Simon!"* In other words, *"By George, you've got it!"* And then Jesus goes on to tell Peter and the other Apostles that it is upon Peter and this confession that He will build the church.

The goal of this piece is to remind you, me and anyone who reads it that as Christians we are to give our lives to Jesus Christ. Another of my mentors, Anglican theologian and pastor, the Reverend John Stott puts it this way:

> *A Christian is somebody personally related to Jesus Christ. Christianity without Christ is a chest without a treasure, a frame without a portrait, a corpse without breath. Christ comes to each of us with an individual summons: "Come to me," "follow me." And the Christian life begins as, however hesitantly and falteringly, we respond to His call. Then as*

> *we start following him, we discover to our increasing and delighted surprise, that a personal relationship to Christ is a many-sided, many-colored, many-splendored thing. We find that he is our mediator and our foundation, our life-giver and our lord, the secret and the goal of our living, our lover and our model... We learn that to be a Christian is to live our lives through, on, in, under, with, unto, for and like Jesus Christ. Each preposition indicates a different kind of relationship, but in each case Christ himself is at the centre.*[1]

As I was preparing this final piece, I realized that it was thirty years ago, almost to the day, when I made this "hesitant and faltering" response of which Stott writes. Thanks to the consistent pressing of my father and mother, church was always part of my life. I was baptized as an infant, grew up in Sunday school, learned the hymns and went to Vacation Bible School and youth group. As a teen, I was confirmed into the church. God was clearly at work in and through all those moments.

But as God comes to us in many ways and makes His children in many varieties, some of us come to God in different ways. Clearly,

1 John R. W. Stott, *Life in Christ* (New York: Tyndale House Publishers, 1991) 111.

ever since I was a child, God had been part of my life, but had I actually decided to follow Him? My answer had to be no.

I began to encounter many people, young and old, who spoke of a relationship with Christ. They described it in all kinds of ways—born again, renewal, commitment, conversion, coming to Christ. For some, it was momentary like a church service or crusade; for others it was a lifetime journey, something that they had simply always known. Some really did make this decision at their Confirmation or Baptism, others like me, did not. Whatever "it" was, I knew I wanted it. I wanted that personal relationship with Christ.

I spent a great deal of time with various clergy those three decades ago. One afternoon, I was sitting by a friend's pool with a campus minister asking all kinds of questions. Finally, with a smile, he said, *"You know, we can sit and ask and answer questions all afternoon, but I think what you are really looking for is a relationship with Christ. Have you made the decision to follow Him?"*

I was honest enough to say, *"You know, I am not sure."* The minister smiled and said, *"Why don't you think about that and then we can get to the questions."* It was a good provoking thought.

I spent the rest of the day reflecting not only on the many times I had conversations in the previous months with people about this relationship I desired. I also spent a great deal of time pondering my religious history. Baptism, *check*. Confirmation, *check*. Sunday school, *check*. Bible reader, *check*. Nightly prayers, *check*. Decision to follow, to really give my life to Christ? *No check*.

That night after supper, I went up to my room, closed my door, got down on my knees and prayed. I cannot tell you at this moment what I prayed or how I prayed it. I only know that I offered my life to Christ, to be a follower, to be a disciple. I wanted not just to say I was a Christian, I wanted to be a Christian.

I remember finishing the prayer with some hope that an angel would appear, music would swell, light would fill the room. Nothing. I got up off my knees and went to bed without any spiritual earthquake whatsoever.

The next morning, as I opened my eyes I noticed one thing—the presence of God. Not a physical presence, just a kind of reality that Jesus was not a historical figure, but was now part of who I was, and I

part of Him; I had been grafted into Him. There has never been a day in my life since that moment that I have not known the presence of Christ in my life.

I was not perfect at that moment nor am I now. There were many things I did, and perhaps have done today, after that moment that did not look at all Christ-like. There have been days when I have been terribly mad or upset with Christ; others when I have doubted Him and His work in my life and the world. There have been days when He has, by my sinful human interpretation, disappointed me, and many more that I have disappointed Him. There have been days when Jesus has shown up where I never expected and days when I thought He would be there, but he never came as I wanted. There have been days when He has felt as far away as the next galaxy and others when He is as close as the bread and wine at Communion. The point is that the relationship began and He has always, always been faithful even when I am not.

I wonder if you have made that decision? Sometimes we need to "re-make it." And really the point is not *how* you do it, but *if* you do it. You do not have to be in any kind of particular place or state of being. Sometimes it is in a moment of terror or after a spiritual encounter, sometimes when you have been really forgiven or moved by injustice in the world, maybe in a religious service or in the privacy of your bedroom. I think the point is just to invite Him in and let Him get to work.

In 1961, Irving Stone wrote a biographical novel, *The Agony and the Ecstasy,* about the life of sculptor Michelangelo Buonarroti. A few years later, a portion of the novel which focused on the painting of the Sistine Chapel was made into a major film starring Charlton Heston as Michelangelo and Rex Harrison as Pope Julius II.

If you know the film, you know there is a great deal of conflict, initially between Michelangelo and the Pope. They haggle over price and design, how long it will take and what the final product will look like. Finally they agree and the artist moves into place.

He sets up his scaffolding and gets to work. Almost from the beginning, Pope Julius, anxious to have a complete product comes into the chapel and yells up to the artist, *"When will you make an end of it!"* And Michelangelo just looks back down, usually with some instrument hanging from his hand or brush from his lips, *"When I am finished!"*

What is he doing? Why is it taking so long? He is patching the holes, filling in the cracks, sanding the rough spots, then he will draw the design, fill it in slowly, deliberately, until it is just right. But every few weeks, in pops the Pope, *"When will you make an end of it!"* The answer, *"When I am finished!"*

As the movie reaches its end, we find both the pope and the artist late in life, both struggling with health issues, both having given so much of themselves to this project. The pope thinks he will not live to see it, but then he rallies. At this point the film's director, Carol Reed, gives his audience an incredible gift.

We see Julius approach the chapel and large, heavy curtains are pulled back. Music swells and no words are spoken—just visions of the beauty created once the artist has been able to move into the chapel and complete his work.

At times, we can be like Pope Julius. We want to be perfect or whole; we want all our questions answered and our doubts wiped away, but it does not work that way. What God says to us in Christ is, *"Just let me move in, let me set up shop; if you trust Me I will get to work. I will patch up the holes, fill in the cracks, sand down the rough spots making you the creature you have always wanted to be. You may get impatient and you may ask Me to finish, but trust Me. If you invite Me in, I am in to stay and I am working, creating a beautiful chapel in you that you may not even see until you slip from this life to the next. But when you do and the curtain is pulled back, what you will find will be a vision you cannot even comprehend."*

I have ended each meditation with a provoking thought and also a prayer from either our Christian tradition or in some cases a prayer I have written. But I will not close that way.

I invite you to come up with your own "Provoking Thought" and your own prayer to respond to it. If you already know and serve our Lord, I pray this book has fed you in some way. If you have a need to step more deeply, then I pray you will do that as well. And if you have yet to invite that great artist within the chapel of your heart, I encourage you to do that today, in your own prayer with your own words.

Well?

Amen.

Scripture Index

Author Index